Bethany Lowe's
Folk Art Halloween

Bethany Lowe's
Folk Art Halloween

LARK BOOKS

A Division of Sterling Publishing Co., Inc.
New York / London

A Red Lips 4 Courage Communications, Inc. book

www.redlips4courage.com

Eileen Cannon Paulin
President
Catherine Risling
Director of Editorial

Book Editor: Rebecca Ittner
Copy Editors: Lecia Monsen, Catherine Risling
Book Designer: Jocelyn Foye
Photographer: Zachary Williams
Stylists: Rebecca Ittner, Catherine Risling

Library of Congress Cataloging-in-Publication Data

Lowe, Bethany.
  Bethany Lowe's / Folk Art Halloween. -- 1st ed.
      p. cm.
  Includes index.
  ISBN-13: 978-1-60059-253-9 (hc-plc with jacket : alk. paper)
  ISBN-10: 1-60059-253-8 (hc-plc with jacket : alk. paper)
  1. Holiday decorations. 2. Handicraft. I. Title.
  TT900.H32L69 2008
  745.594'1646--dc22

                            2007046184

10 9 8 7 6 5 4 3 2 1

First Edition

Published by Lark Books, A Division of Sterling Publishing Co., Inc.
387 Park Avenue South, New York, NY 10016

Distributed in Canada by Sterling Publishing,
c/o Canadian Manda Group, 165 Dufferin St.
Toronto, Ontario, Canada M6K 3H6

Distributed in the United Kingdom by GMC Distribution Services,
Castle Place, 166 High St., Lewes, East Sussex, England BN7 1XU

Distributed in Australia by Capricorn Link (Australia) Pty Ltd.,
P.O. Box 704, Windsor, NSW 2756 Australia

If you have questions or comments about this book, please contact:
Lark Books
67 Broadway
Asheville, NC 28801
(828) 253-0467

Manufactured in China

For information about custom editions, special sales, premium and corporate purchases, please contact Sterling Special Sales Department at (800) 805-5489 or specialsales@sterlingpub.com.

Dedication

This book is dedicated to my stoic and steadfast husband, Curt, who puts up with my crazy, creative ideas and never-ending search for more old stuff. He now brakes for antique shops without my having to ask. Together we have created a business that has provided a life filled with unexpected travels and new, amazing friends all over the world. Curt, you are the wind beneath my wings.

To my parents, Mae and Bill, who made our home and family holidays so very special. Mom taught me that homemade was often better than store bought. Dad gave me a love of history and tradition and showed me that if you are passionate about something that you can turn it into your life's work, no matter how unusual it is.

Contents

Halloween Memories

Halloween was an especially magical time for my family and has been one of my favorite holidays since I was a child. In the small farming community where I grew up, children dressed in homemade Halloween costumes and went trick-or-treating door-to-door. Every year our community hosted a Halloween party for the children where we carved pumpkins, bobbed for apples, played Halloween games, and had costume contests.

When my older brother and I went trick-or-treating as grade-schoolers, we covered the entire town. Every house on the block had the welcome light on and was decorated to greet the greedy youngsters in search of goodies.

Carving pumpkins was something that our entire family did together. Not only did we carve a face, but my mother also taught us to use gumdrops, licorice, and other candies to create accessories for our pumpkins, such as earrings, lips, eyebrows, and so forth. Hats for the pumpkins were constructed from old newspapers or wrapping paper. Our pumpkins were not just pumpkins; they became magical Halloween characters to light up the night.

Remembering back to the costumes I wore as a child, the silliest ones had to have been the Mr. and Mrs. Potato Head my younger brother and I were forced to wear. My mother thought the outfits were outstanding, but at age 6, I was totally horrified. I wore my favorite costume at age 9. I went as a one-eyed-purple-people-eater, which also happened to be the most popular song that year. My mother sewed the costume based on my original drawings. My creativity probably comes from my mother, who sewed all these early costumes.

My love for Halloween design stems from my ability to capture this whimsical holiday with fresh and original ideas. More than any other holiday, Halloween encourages me to venture down many avenues of interpretation. Halloween is the one holiday that allows adults to become children again. It is the time of the year that we are all willing to dress up and make fools of ourselves.

Halloween themes are many and varied— from spooky and scary to whimsical or sweet. Halloween parties encourage friends and family to gather together for a good time, fun treats, and lots of laughs. My vintage look is inspired by my passion for anything old with a story to tell.

In recent years, Halloween has become one of the most celebrated holidays. I began creating Halloween collectibles because there were no high-quality Halloween designs in the market with a vintage feel. Collectors were limited to buying authentic vintage pieces—which are expensive and fragile. I wanted to decorate my own home with unique folk art-style Halloween décor, and I knew other people felt the same way. I decided to create them myself. Papier-mâché buckets, candy containers, and tin lanterns were some of my earliest vintage designs. At this time, I also began making wool appliquéd pillows, table runners, and ornaments in a Halloween theme. We used hand-dyed wool and stitched the projects completely by hand.

I hope the ideas found in this book will awaken the charming whimsy of your past. Think back to your favorite Halloween costume as a child. Relive your first time trick-or-treating.

I have introduced new ideas and combined them with vintage memorabilia to help you build a tradition for your family and friends to celebrate for years to come. In addition, all of the images, templates, and patterns needed to complete the projects have been provided. Happy haunting this Halloween!

Bethany Lowe

Chapter 1

Getting Started

People always ask me, "What is folk art?" I define folk art as art created by someone who has no formal or academic artistic training, but whose works are part of an established tradition of style and craftsmanship. A folk artist's direct and honest depiction of subjects usually reflects social and cultural characteristics. Simple flat figures, bright colors, and unlikely spatial relationships often characterize folk designs.

I am a self-taught artist, which frees me from the constraints of formal art training. I often approach my artwork in unconventional ways and with uncommon methods. I actually cannot follow patterns or other artist's instructions very well. It seems I am always taking a shortcut to achieve the end results. This can result in many "do-overs"—something I have never been afraid of. You can learn a lot through a do-over, so don't ever be afraid to try something new. Perfection is not a word that defines folk art.

The projects in this book are made using a variety of crafting techniques, from paper crafting, sewing, and embroidery to sculpting and woodworking. I have tried to include designs that interest every level of crafter or folk artist.

Through years of making original folk art designs, I have come up with this list of the materials and tools I use most often. You will find throughout the project instructions that I use very basic materials—nothing too fancy. I use time-honored techniques and tools, keeping the process of creating simple and enjoyable.

Always read the instructions of any product prior to using it. Then, test the product on a scrap piece of material before applying it to your project.

Remember, mistakes happen. If this occurs, don't fret. Use your imagination. Sometimes the worst mistakes can be manipulated to your advantage with stunning results.

Materials & Tools

Adhesives

In my tool box you will find a host of adhesives including craft glue, Cyanoacrylate glue (this is quick-drying, strong-hold glue), a hot glue gun and glue sticks, decoupage medium, rubber cement, and spray adhesives. I also use a variety of tapes including cellophane, double-sided, and florist's tape.

Clay

Two types of clay are used for the projects in this book: paper clay and polymer clay. Paper clay is a white modeling material that air-dries to a hard finish. It can be molded, sculpted, or shaped while it is moist and easily adheres to many surfaces. Polymer clay is available in a wide variety of colors, and it is easily molded, sculpted, and shaped. Polymer clay does require baking to harden. Both types of clay can be painted, sanded, and embellished once they are dry. Always follow the manufacturer's instructions when working with clay.

Embellishments

I use embellishments to dress up most everything I create. I used my favorite embellishments on the projects found here including beads, buttons, garland, glitter, vintage jewelry pieces, pipe cleaners, and tinsel.

Fabric, Sewing, and Stitching Supplies

To complete the sewn and embroidered projects, you will need to have some simple fabric supplies on hand, including batting, cotton fabric, wool, and tulle. For sewing and stitching you will need a sewing machine and assorted needles, including beading, chenille, crochet, doll-making, embroidery, machine, and hand sewing. You also will need straight pins. Thread types needed include crochet, embroidery, hand and machine sewing, and upholstery.

Forms, Wooden Items, and Wire Supplies

There is a host of pre-made crafting forms and supplies and everyday items that you will need to complete the projects in this book. You can easily find these items in art and craft stores. They include polystyrene foam balls, plastic masks, and papier-mâché forms such as a boot, nesting boxes, and trunks. Other items you will need include plywood, wooden dowels and skewers, and wooden toothpicks. Wire items needed include craft wire in a variety of sizes and a wire wreath form.

Lace, Fringe, and Ribbon

Lace, fringe, and ribbon can be used to dress up your folk art creations, as well as to tie things together. I love using vintage items, though it is perfectly acceptable to use modern versions. You can find the types needed for the projects in this book at your local craft store.

Paint and Painting Supplies

You will use acrylic paint and spray paint on many of the projects. In addition you will want to have on hand: paintbrushes in a variety of sizes; a paint palette; antiquing glaze, to add interest to sculpted projects; and spray sealer, to protect finished items. Always work in a well-ventilated area when using paints and glazes.

Paper Crafting Supplies

The projects featured in the following chapters use a variety of easy-to-find papers including cardstock, crepe paper, copy paper, iron-on transfer paper, and vellum. Other paper items include invitations and envelopes, picture mats, and paper tubes.

Tools

All the projects require basic tools such as a craft knife, scissors (including craft, decorative-edge, and embroidery), paper punches, pinking shears, screwdrivers, and wire cutters.

Additional items necessary
to complete the projects:
• Computer and printer or color copier
• Iron and ironing surface
• Sandpaper
• Spray bottle
• Tea bags

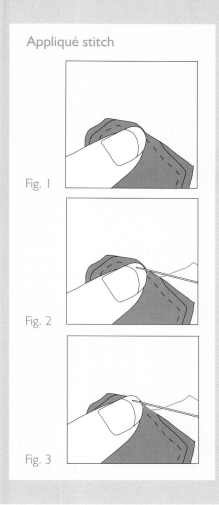

Appliqué stitch

Fig. 1

Fig. 2

Fig. 3

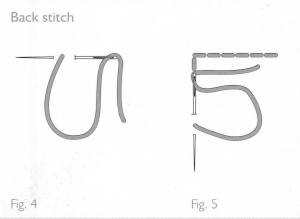

Back stitch

Fig. 4　　　　　Fig. 5

Stitches and Knots

Appliqué stitch

Using 100-percent cotton thread that matches the color of the appliqué shape, thread a needle with a single 15-inch (38.1 cm) strand, knotting the end with a quilter's knot (page 20).

Using the tip of your needle, turn a seam allowance under, along the drawn line. Fold under a 1-inch (2.5 cm) section, using the thumb on your non-sewing hand to press the seam as you sew. Start your first stitch with the knot tucked under the appliqué shape. This will prevent the thread from showing (see fig. 1).

Push the needle through the background fabric right next to the appliqué shape, and then come up about ⅛ inch (0.3 cm) ahead, grabbing only a couple of threads on the edge of the appliqué shape (see fig. 2).

Push the needle back into the background fabric right next to the previous stitch, keeping the stitch as close to the appliqué shape as possible without going through it (see fig. 3).

Continue in this manner around the entire appliqué, using the point and side of the needle to turn the edges under as you go. To prevent puckering, be careful not to pull the thread too tight as you stitch. The shape should lie flat.

Back stitch

Bring the needle up through the fabric and reinsert it back down through the fabric (see fig. 4), making a stitch of desired length. Repeat (see fig. 5).

Blanket stitch

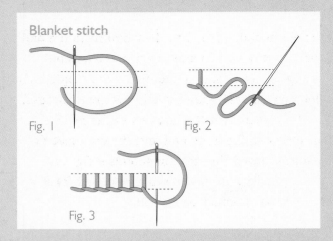

Fig. 1

Fig. 2

Fig. 3

Chain stitch

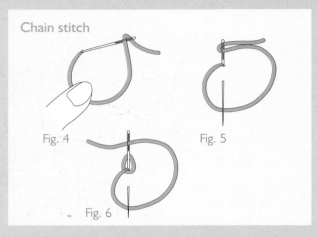

Fig. 4

Fig. 5

Fig. 6

Couching stitch

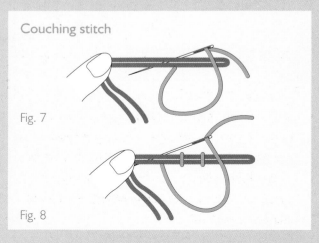

Fig. 7

Fig. 8

Blanket stitch

Bring the needle to the front on the lower line, and then insert the needle at the top, a bit to the right. Bring the needle out directly below, making sure to keep the thread under the tip of the needle (see fig. 1).

Pull the thread through the fabric, over the top of the working thread. Pull the thread to form a firm loop at the lower line (see fig. 2). Continue on, making sure to space the stitches evenly and at the same height (see fig. 3).

Chain stitch

Bring the needle up through the fabric and make a loop. Reinsert the needle right next to the emerging thread (see fig. 4), and bring the needle back out, to the front of the fabric so the needle point is over the thread (see fig. 5). Repeat to make a chain of desired length (see fig. 6).

Couching stitch

Bring the needle with the laid thread up from the back of the fabric to the front and hold it in place with your thumb. Use the working thread to secure the laid thread to the fabric (see fig. 7). Push the needle with the laid thread to the back of the fabric and secure. Continue on (see fig. 8).

Crochet stitch

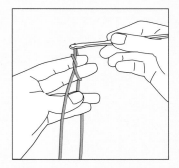

Fig. 9

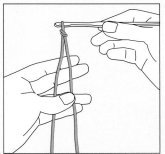

Fig. 10

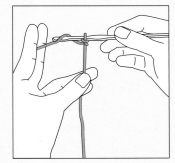

Fig. 11

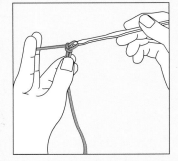

Fig. 12

Crochet stitch

Begin the chain about 6 inches (15.2 cm) from the end of the thread. Make a slip knot around the crochet hook (see fig. 9). *Note:* A slip knot is a loose single knot with a loop just large enough to slip the hook through.

Wrap the thread over the hook from the back to the front between the hook end and the knot (see fig. 10). Bring the thread through the loop (see fig. 11). Repeat to make the number of stitches called for in the pattern instructions (see fig. 12).

Finding Fabrics

Take advantage of the selection at your local craft and fabric stores when looking for your fabrics. Or, rummage through closets and attics to find fabric you have on hand. Remember, it's supposed to look old. Grandmothers are a great source for material.

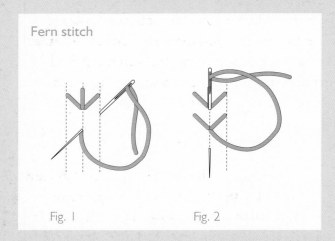

Fern stitch

Fig. 1   Fig. 2

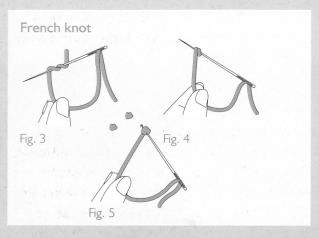

French knot

Fig. 3   Fig. 4

Fig. 5

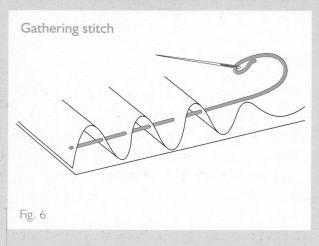

Gathering stitch

Fig. 6

Fern stitch

Create the fern stitch with three straight stitches of equal length, each originating at the same point. After the group of three stitches is completed, bring the needle down through an equal distance, beginning the next group of stitches (see fig. 1). Continue on (see fig. 2).

French knot

Work two tiny stitches at the back of the fabric, and then bring the thread through to the front of the fabric. Hold the thread taut and wrap it two or three times around the needle (see fig. 3). Pull on the thread to gently tighten the twists (see fig. 4). While holding the thread taut, reinsert the needle into the fabric, close to the point where it emerged. Pull the needle and thread to the back of the fabric, leaving a loose knot at the front (see fig. 5). Work two tiny stitches on the back to tie off.

Gathering stitch

On some garments, one piece of fabric is larger than the piece to which it will be joined. In order to sew the seam, the larger fabric edge must be gathered until its length matches the shorter fabric edge. You can sew gathering stitches by hand or by machine.

To gather the longer edge by hand, sew a series of loose, evenly spaced running stitches, putting tension on the thread so the fabric bunches or gathers between stitches (see fig. 6). The tension will determine the size of the gathers while the number of stitches will determine the number of gathers. When the gathered edge matches the length of the other edge, the fabric pieces can be pinned and sewn as with other seams.

Herringbone stitch

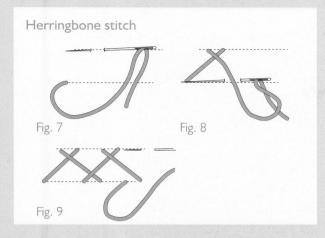

Fig. 7

Fig. 8

Fig. 9

Lazy daisy stitch

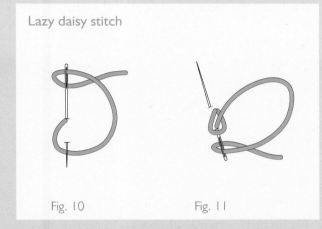

Fig. 10

Fig. 11

Overhand stitch

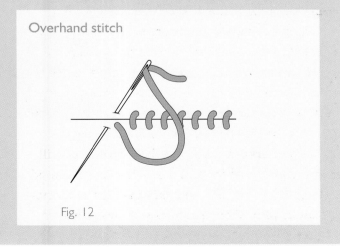

Fig. 12

To gather a piece by machine, sew two rows of parallel stitching and pull the upper thread to gather. (Two rows of stitches provide back-up if a thread breaks.) Increase the tension on the sewing machine to make the gathering easier.

Herringbone stitch

Bring the thread out on the lower line at the left side and insert it on the upper line a little to the right, taking a small stitch to the left (see fig. 7). Insert the needle on the lower line a bit to the right and take a small stitch to the left (see fig. 8). Repeat, making sure that the stitches are of equal size and are evenly spaced (see fig. 9).

Lazy daisy stitch

Bring the needle through to the front of the fabric. Reinsert the needle right next to the emerging thread, and back out to the front again, one stitch length away and with the working thread under the needle point (see fig. 10). Pull the thread so the loop stays flat, and make a short, straight stitch over the loop to anchor it (see fig. 11).

Overhand stitch

Insert the needle diagonally from the back edge of the fabric through to the front edge, picking up only one or two threads of fabric each time. Reinsert the needle directly behind the previous stitch and bring it back through one stitch length away (see fig. 12).

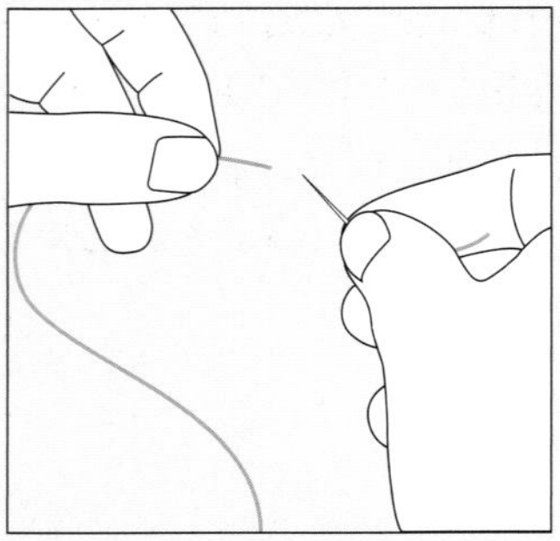

Fig. 1

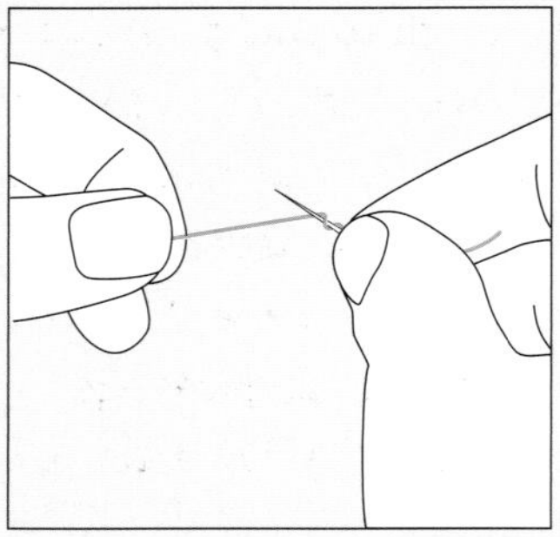

Fig. 2

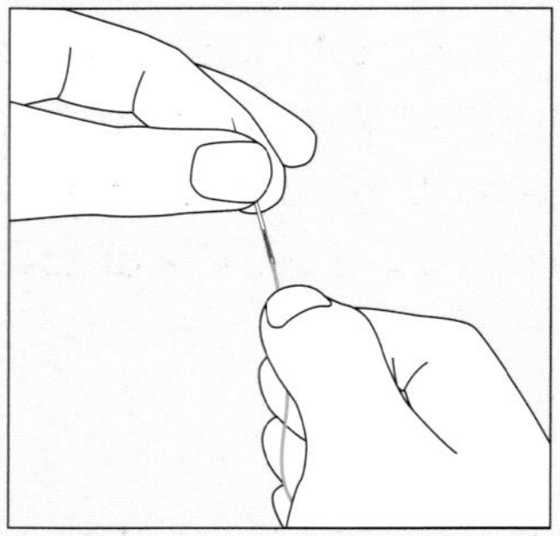

Fig. 3

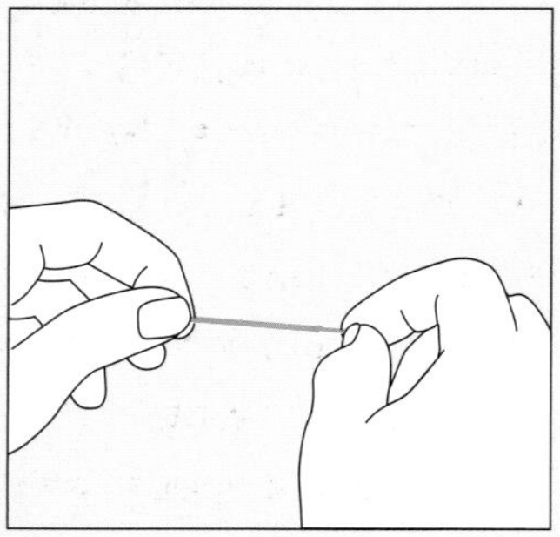

Fig. 4

Quilter's knot

Thread the needle. (You will be using a single thread for sewing.) Hold the end of the thread in your left hand and the needle in your right hand. Point the end of the thread at the point of the needle (see fig. 1).

Lay the needle over the end of the thread, taking hold of the thread with the right thumb and index finger. Wrap the thread around the needle about three times—more if a larger knot is desired (see fig. 2).

Carefully slide the wrapped thread in between the thumb and index finger of the right hand. Don't let go (see fig. 3). Take hold of the point of the needle with the left hand thumb and index finger and, keeping hold of the knotted area, pull gently all the way along the thread until you feel the knot at the end (see fig. 4). Reverse the instructions if you are left handed.

Tips & Tricks

Finding Inspiration

Some of my favorite sources for Halloween images and inspirations include:

- *antique buttons, trims, and fabrics*
- *antique shows or malls*
- *children's pictures*
- *flea markets*
- *Halloween books*
- *old family albums*
- *old Halloween costumes and games*
- *The Dennison's Bogie Books from the early 1900s*
- *vintage children's books*
- *vintage postcards*

Running stitch

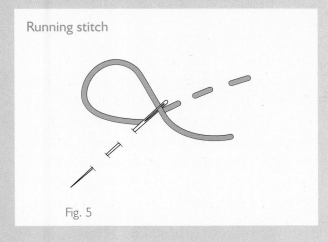

Fig. 5

Satin stitch

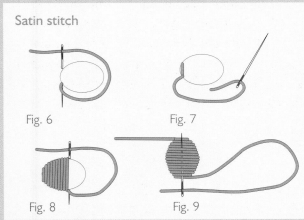

Fig. 6

Fig. 7

Fig. 8

Fig. 9

Slip stitch

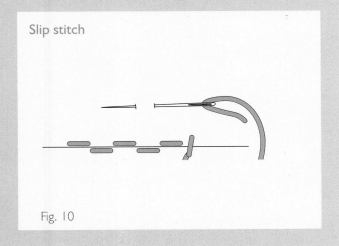

Fig. 10

Running stitch

Bring the needle up through the fabric and pass it in and out of the fabric along the desired stitch line, keeping the stitch lengths and spaces between the stitches even (see fig. 5). Reinsert the needle back through the fabric and tie off.

Satin stitch

Bring the needle through to the front of the fabric at the edge of the shape to be filled in. Insert the needle at the opposite edge of the shape, and then bring it out again next to where you began (see fig. 6). Pull the thread gently to straighten it out. The thread should lie smoothly without puckering (see fig. 7). Continue in the same manner, keeping the stitches even and close together (see fig. 8).

When you have finished filling in the shape, push the needle to the back of the fabric and weave the thread through the back of your stitching (see fig. 9). Snip the thread close to the surface of the stitching.

Slip stitch

A slip stitch is a nearly invisible hand stitch used to close openings and finish sewing projects.

Thread your needle, then bring the needle up and through one edge. Working from right to left, slip the needle through the edge of the opposite edge, bring the needle out about ¼-inch (0.6 cm) down, and draw the thread through. Continue along, slipping the needle and thread through the opposite edges of the fabric (see fig. 10).

Chapter 2

Haunted Mansion Home Décor

Whether you plan to host a houseful of guests or just welcome trick-or-treaters, you can easily convert your home into a stylish haunt that will bring out the spirits of the season. Postcard images are an easy way to add a charming, vintage touch to your Halloween décor.

Historians consider the "Golden Era" of holiday postcards to span 1906 to 1917, and vintage Halloween postcards are some of the most valuable and sought after by collectors. Halloween art depicted family fun, fantasy, and a spooky good time rather than being dark or scary. Jack-o-lanterns, witches, black cats, laughing moon faces, owls, and children are some of the most popular images on Halloween post-cards that were created by the best artists of the period. Orange and black were the predominant colors used as they represented two major symbols of Halloween, jack-o-lanterns and the night.

The projects shown in this chapter feature some of my favorite vintage postcard images. Use the images I have provided, or choose some of your own.

Tinsel Tree in Witch's Boot
with Paper Cones and
Postcard Ornaments

Feather trees were introduced in the late 1800s as a Christmas decoration. I borrowed this wonderful vintage tabletop idea to fashion a stunning tinsel-top tree for your Halloween setting. By using metallic orange and black tinsel with a witch's boot base, you can create a beautiful centerpiece that sets a festive mood when your guests enter the room. Holiday trees are fun to decorate with vintage paper cones and postcard ornaments.

Tinsel Tree in Witch's Boot

The wired branches of this tree are sturdy enough to hold the cones and ornaments without bending. The boot harkens memories of Halloween fairy tales, and is weighted to hold the tinsel tree without tipping.

Instructions

To Make the Witch's Boot

1 Using paper clay, widen the heel and the base of the witch's boot; let dry. Paint the boot and the wooden base with black latex paint; let dry. Using hot glue, adhere the boot to the center of the wooden base.

2 Brush the outer edge of the wooden base and around the boot with paper glue then sprinkle with glitter. *Note:* The glue around the boot is quite haphazard.

To Make the Tinsel Tree

1 Using the wire cutters, cut the wire for the branches as follows: Top Row: four 4-inch (10.2 cm) lengths; Row 2: four 5-inch (12.7 cm) lengths; Row 3: four 5½-inch (14 cm) lengths; Row 4: five 7-inch (17.8 cm) lengths, Row 5: five 7½-inch (19.1 cm) lengths; Row 6: six 8½-inch (21.6 cm) lengths; Row 7: six 9-inch (22.9 cm) lengths; Row 8: seven 10-inch (25.4 cm) lengths.

2 Using pliers, make a 90-degree bend in each wire 2 inches (5.1 cm) from one end.

3 Wrap each wire from end to end with floral tape. Keep each row together. Wrap each wire with both colors of wired tinsel garland. Secure the ends of the tinsel garland with hot glue. *Note*: Do not wrap the 2-inch (5.1 cm) end with tinsel.

4 Starting with the top row, use cellophane tape to fasten the rows of branches to the dowel, spacing the rows evenly around the dowel. *Note*: The rows will be loose, but the cellophane tape will hold the wire and keep the rows spaced evenly before they are wrapped with floral tape.

5 Wrap the top row well with floral tape, and then wrap floral tape around ¾ inch (1.9 cm) of the dowel below each row. *Note*: This is now the top branch.

6 Attach remaining branches row by row, spacing evenly around the dowel with cellophane tape. Securely wrap floral tape over the cellophane tape. *Note*: Each row is approximately 2¾ inches (7 cm) below previous row.

7 Continue wrapping floral tape around until you reach the end of the dowel. Brush any visible floral tape with acrylic paint.

Materials

- Acrylic paint: black
- Buckle
- Craft wire: 22-gauge
- Crepe paper: black
- Glitter: black
- Glue: craft, paper
- Latex paint: black
- Paper clay
- Papier-mâché boot
- Plastic bag: gallon size
- Quick-setting gypsum plaster
- Ribbon: black, 1½ inches (3.8 cm) wide (3 yards [2.74 meters])
- Tape: cellophane, floral
- Thread: black
- Tinsel garland: wired black, wired orange (15 yards [13.71 meters] each color)
- Wooden base: 8-inch (20.3 cm) square
- Wooden dowel: ½ x 30 inches (1.3 x 76.2 cm)

Tools

- Craft scissors
- Hot glue gun and glue sticks
- Needle
- Paintbrush
- Pliers
- Ruler
- Wire cutters

To Secure the Tree in the Witch's Boot

1 Mix quick-setting gypsum plaster according to package directions. Pour 1½ cups (360 ml) of plaster into the plastic bag. Ease the plastic bag into the boot, with the bag opening at the top of the boot.

2 Place the bottom of the tree into the plaster, making sure the tree is straight. Allow the plaster to dry.

To Embellish the Witch's Boot

1 Cut one 4 x 12-inch (10.2 x 30.5 cm) strip of crepe paper. Using a needle and thread, gather the strip, accordion-style, and hot glue the bottom edge to the inside top of the boot.

2 Tie the ribbon around the boot and make a bow. Secure the ribbon in place with hot glue. Place the buckle on the ribbon and secure it with hot glue.

Tips & Tricks

Hot Glue Tips

Be careful when using a hot glue gun. The tool and glue are extremely hot and can burn you. Do not let children use this tool on any project they are working on. Also, remember to use the glue sparingly.

Vintage Postcard Ornaments

These ornaments add spirit to a tabletop tree or table setting when used as napkin rings. This is a delightfully easy project with a true vintage look.

Materials

- Cardstock: white, 8½ x 11 inches (21.6 x 27.9 cm)
- Matboard
- Ribbon: black, ¼-inch (0.6 cm) wide (2 inches [5.1 cm] per ornament)
- Rubber cement
- String
- Tinsel pipe cleaners: silver

Tools

- Computer and printer or color copier
- Craft knife
- Craft scissors
- Cutting mat
- Hot glue gun and glue sticks
- Paintbrush: small
- Ruler
- Sandpaper

Instructions

1. Using the craft knife, cutting mat, and ruler cut the matboard into 2 x 3-inch (5.1 x 7.6 cm) rectangles. Gently sand the edges of the rectangles.

2. Copy the Cones and Ornaments images (page 102–103) onto cardstock. Cut out the images with craft scissors. Using the paintbrush, apply rubber cement on both sides of a piece of matboard and adhere an image to each side.

3. Hot glue a tinsel pipe cleaner around the edges of the ornament. Slip a 4-inch (10.2 cm) length of string under the tinsel pipe cleaner at the top of the ornament, then hot glue in place. Embellish with a small black ribbon bow hot glued to the string.

Trick-or-Treat Cones

Cornucopia candy containers originated as Christmas ornaments during the Victorian era. In this project, I designed these cornucopias as mini trick-or-treat cones to decorate the tinsel tree and to give away as party favors. You can also use them to embellish place settings at a Halloween party, feature them in a wreath, or hang them from a garland.

Instructions

1 Copy the Cone template (page 104) onto construction paper and cut out. Using a small paintbrush, apply rubber cement ¼ inch (0.6 cm) in from the edge all along the construction paper. Glue the cone together. Hold the top edges of the cone together with a paper clip until dry.

2 Punch a hole in each side of the cone, about ½ inch (1.3 cm) down from top edge.

3   Twist one orange and one black chenille pipe cleaner together. Thread one end of the twisted piece through each hole and twist the ends together to hold securely.

4   Thread 2 inches (5.1 cm) of wire through the top of the jingle bell. Twist the wire, leaving a small open loop on the end so the bell is slightly loose. Insert the pointed end of the wire into the bottom of the cone and add a dab of rubber cement; let dry.

5   Cut one 1¼ x 18-inch (3.2 x 45.7 cm) strip of crepe paper. Gather the crepe paper, accordion-style, and stitch the gathers in place using the needle and thread and a basting stitch. Hot glue the ruffle to the inside rim of the cone.

6   Cut one ¾ x 3-inch (1.9 x 7.6 cm) strip of crepe paper. Gather the crepe paper, accordion-style, and stitch the gathers in place using the needle and thread and a basting stitch. Hot glue the ruffle to the bottom of the cone.

7   Twist one orange and one black chenille pipe cleaner together. Wrap the twisted piece around the top rim of the cone and hot glue in place.

8   Copy the Cones and Ornament images (page 102–103) onto cardstock. Choose the desired image, trim the edges, and adhere it to the cone with rubber cement.

9   Using a small paintbrush, add rubber cement around the edge of the image and sprinkle with glitter; let dry.

Materials

- Cardstock: white, 8½ x 11 inches (21.6 x 27.9 cm)
- Construction paper: orange
- Craft wire: 24-gauge
- Crepe paper: black
- Glitter: fine black
- Jingle bells: small (1 per cone)
- Paper clips
- Pencil
- Pipe cleaners: black, orange chenille
- Rubber cement
- Thread: black

Tools

- Computer and printer or color copier
- Craft scissors
- Hole punch
- Hot glue gun and glue sticks
- Needle
- Paintbrush: small
- Ruler

Tips & Tricks

Add Vintage Flair to Paper Cones

For a vintage look, use wire tinsel instead of chenille pipe cleaners to create the handle on the cone. Though orange construction paper was used for the cones shown here, any decorative paper would work.

Smiling Jack Tablecloth
with Haunted Images
Table Scarf

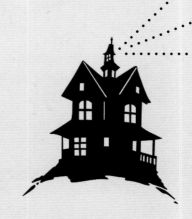

This floor-length Smiling Jack Tablecloth provides the underskirt for the Haunted Images Table Scarf. A crepe paper tablecloth shown in the 1916 Dennison's Bogie Book inspired the jack-o-lantern faces. When topped with the Haunted Images Table Scarf, this party table captures the spirit of Halloween. Its magic comes from vintage postcard images of trick-or-treating children that circle its edge. A charming table is the ambition of every hostess.

Smiling Jack Tablecloth

Materials

- 🎃 Fabric: Halloween-themed at least 45 inches (114.3 cm) wide (7½ yards [6.86 meters])
- 🎃 Fringe: black, 2½ inches (6.4 cm) wide (8 yards [7.32 meters])
- 🎃 Thread: black

Tools

- 🎃 Craft scissors
- 🎃 Fabric chalk
- 🎃 Iron
- 🎃 Sewing machine
- 🎃 Straight pins
- 🎃 Tape measure

Instructions

1. Cut fabric into four equal-sized wedges, each with a 90-degree angle at the top and 45½ (115.6 cm) inches down each side. Do not cut the bottom edge as it will need to be rounded.

2. Using a straight pin, fasten the end of the tape measure to the center point of the fabric. *Note:* The tape measure needs to rotate as you make chalk marks.

3. Using fabric chalk, mark a line 45½ inches (115.6 cm) down from the center point all along the bottom of the fabric. *Note:* This will form the rounded base of your tablecloth.

4. Using a ¼-inch (0.6 cm) seam, stitch two wedges together to form a half circle. Add a third wedge, and then a fourth wedge. Stitch the last side seams together.

5. Press the seams open and sew a ¼-inch (0.6 cm) hem around the bottom edge to prevent the fabric from fraying. Sew on the fringe, making sure to cover the hem with the top of the fringe.

Tips & Tricks

Design Ideas

The pattern for the Smiling Jack Tablecloth is based on using fabric that has a one-way design. If the fabric you choose has a left-to-right pattern, make certain the triangular wedges are cut on the same lines of the design so when they are sewn together the pattern forms one line.

Haunted Images Table Scarf

Materials

- 🎃 Cotton fabric: tan (2 yards [1.83 meters]), black (1¼ yards [1.14 meters])
- 🎃 Iron-on transfer paper
- 🎃 Thread

Tools

- 🎃 Computer and printer or color copier
- 🎃 Craft scissors
- 🎃 Iron
- 🎃 Measuring tape
- 🎃 Sewing machine
- 🎃 Straight pins

Instructions

1 Cut four 11¼ x 72-inch (28.6 x 182.9 cm) strips from tan fabric. *Note:* These strips will create the border of the table scarf.

2 Cut one 44-inch (111.8 cm) square from black fabric. *Note:* This is the center of the table scarf.

3 Using a ¼-inch (0.6 cm) seam, sew the tan strips to the black square, leaving a ¼-inch (0.6 cm) opening at each corner.

4 Miter the corners of the tan strips, pinning them together to form a seam. Using a ¼-inch (0.6 cm) seam, stitch the corners together. Press the seams flat.

5 Stitch a 2-inch (5.1 cm) hem around the edge of the scarf. *Note:* When finished, this piece measures 43 inches (109.2 cm) square.

6 Using a computer and printer, follow the manufacturer's directions to make iron-on transfers of the Haunted Table Scarf images (page 103) and to adhere the images to the table scarf.

Celebrating Box

I have a collection of vintage hatboxes and I find them so handy as a place to stash my stuff—and as a collector, I have plenty of stuff! For this project my friend, Bonnie, used a papier-mâché hatbox and covered it with vintage postcard images and pretty ribbon.

Instructions

1 Using orange spray paint, paint the inside and outside of the box lid and the box bottom; let dry. Using black spray paint, lightly spray the box bottom.

2 Copy the Celebrating Box images (page 107) onto cardstock. Trim the images and apply decoupage medium to the back of each one with the foam brush, then place the images on the box as desired.

3 Cut a length of ribbon to go around the lid of the box. Attach the ribbon to the lid using the paintbrush and rubber cement.

4 Cut two 4 x 18-inch (10.2 x 45.7 cm) strips of orange crepe paper, and two same-size strips of black crepe paper. Fringe each piece by cutting up from the 18-inch (45.7 cm) side, cutting to within ½ inch (1.3 cm) of the opposite edge.

5 Lay the orange crepe paper on top of the black crepe paper and tightly roll from the 4-inch (10.2 cm) side. Fasten the roll with cellophane tape, and then fluff the crepe paper.

6 Fashion a bow from the wired ribbon. Using hot glue, attach the crepe paper tassels and the bow to the lid.

Materials

- Cardstock: white, 8½ x 10 inches (21.6 x 25.4 cm) (6)
- Cellophane tape
- Crepe paper: black, orange
- Decoupage medium: matte finish
- Papier-mâché box and lid: oval-shaped, 9¾ x 7½ x 8 inches (24.8 x 19.1 x 20.3 cm)
- Ribbon: wired, 1½ inches (3.8 cm) wide (2½ yards [2.29 meters])
- Rubber cement
- Spray paint: black, orange

Tools

- Computer and printer or color copier
- Craft scissors
- Foam brush
- Hot glue gun and glue sticks
- Paintbrush: small
- Pencil
- Ruler

Tips & Tricks

Creating Paint Effects

Use a light touch when spraying black paint over the orange-painted box bottom. It should just be an overspray. You also can use black webbing spray to create an interesting textured look on the box bottom.

Celebration Wreath

This fast-and-easy wreath is at home on the front door to greet trick-or-treaters, or on a wall to welcome the fall season. A glittered papier-mâché hat adds just the right amount of sparkle. This is great project for your leftover ribbons.

Instructions

1. Cut the ribbons into 7½-inch (19.1 cm) lengths using pinking shears. *Note:* You will need approximately 200 cut pieces of ribbon to create a full-looking wreath.

2. Beginning in the center of the wreath form, tie the ribbons side by side around the form. *Note:* One loop will hold each ribbon securely. To create a full-looking wreath, slide the knots close together.

3. Continue this process to the outer edge of the wreath form, one wire circle at a time.

4. Drop the tea bags into 3 quarts of boiling water and steep until very dark; let cool. Fill the spray bottle with tea and spray the tea onto the wreath; let dry.

5. Spray the papier-mâché witch's hat with adhesive, and then cover it with glitter; let dry. Tie the hat to the wreath with craft wire. Embellish the hat with a spider web.

Tips & Tricks

Tea-Stained to Perfection

Tea staining will give any project a vintage look. To tea stain fabric or lace, bring water to a boil in an open pan then turn off the heat. Add 2 to 3 family-sized tea bags per gallon of boiled water. Submerge your fabric, lace, or ribbons in the tea solution for 20 minutes. If they turn too dark you can always rinse out some of the color until you attain the shade you desire. I prefer a heavier, uneven color that looks like fabric aged in an attic. You can achieve a lighter tea-stained effect by spraying a finished project with the tea solution. Make sure to cover any areas that you do not want sprayed.

Materials

- Adhesive spray
- Craft wire: 22-gauge
- Glitter: black
- Papier-mâché witch's hat
- Ribbons: assorted colors and widths (40–45 yards [36.58–41.15 meters])
- Spider web embellishment
- Tea bags: large (10)
- Wire wreath form: 12-inch (30.5 cm)

Tools

- Pinking shears
- Spray bottle
- Wire cutters

Party Poppers

Holiday poppers originated
in England as Christmas party
favors filled with candies or
prizes for each guest. When
pulled to open, a loud popping
sound was made and the guest
received their prize. The vintage
poppers could be used only
once. These poppers are made
as party favors that can be used
again and again.

Instructions

1 Cut four 6 x 10-inch (15.2 x 25.4 cm) rectangles from orange crepe paper. Brush rubber cement over the exterior of each PVC pipe piece and down into the ends of the pipe. Wrap a crepe paper rectangle around each pipe, and then tuck the ends of the paper inside the ends. Press firmly into place; let dry.

2 Cut sixteen 3 x 31-inch (7.6 x 78.7 cm) strips of orange crepe paper. Cut a ¼-inch- (0.6 cm) wide fringe on eight of the strips.

3 Gently roll one strip of the uncut crepe paper starting on the short end, pinching at the bottom. Roll one strip of fringe around the rolled uncut paper, pinching the bottom tightly. Wrap the piece with wire. Fluff the fringe. This will make one tassel end. Repeat for remaining seven ends.

4 Cut sixteen 4-inch (10.2 cm) circles from orange crepe paper. Tightly wad a small piece of newspaper into a ball about ¾ inch (1.9 cm) tall by the width of the PVC pipe. This will slip in and out of the ends of your pipe like a stopper. Place the wad of newspaper in the center of a double thickness of 4-inch (10.2 cm) circles. Bring the side of the circle around the newspaper. Pinch the opening closed so it will have a shape. Open this area, squirt hot glue liberally onto the packed newspaper, and set the tassel onto the hot glue. Bring the sides of the 4-inch (10.2 cm) circle around the tassel base and tie with craft wire. The ends should easily slip into the PVC pipe.

5 Copy the Checkerboard Paper (page 108) and Party Popper images (page 104) onto cardstock and cut them out. Using a small paintbrush, apply rubber cement onto each popper and adhere the paper and images. Fill as desired then tie the ends of the poppers with ribbon.

Materials

- Cardstock: white, 8½ x 10 inches (21.6 x 25.4 cm)
- Craft wire: 24-gauge
- Crepe paper: orange
- Newspaper
- PVC pipe: 1½ x 3¾ inches (3.8 x 9.5 cm) (4)
- Ribbon
- Rubber cement

Tools

- Computer and printer or color copier
- Craft scissors
- Hot glue gun and glue sticks
- Paintbrush: small
- Ruler

Tips & Tricks

PVC-Free Poppers

The party poppers can also be made using empty bathroom tissue cylinders. Just adjust the measurements of the crepe paper used to cover them.

Tassel Masks

These fun paper-and-glitter masks were inspired by 1920s-era Halloween-themed plumed hats. Created by my assistant designer, Wendy, the masks provide instant costumes for party guests, or they can be used to decorate a pumpkin. The masks also make great centerpieces.

Instructions

1 Copy the Cat and Pumpkin Mask and Nose templates (page 105) and Cat and Pumpkin Mask Toppers templates (page 106) onto cardstock; cut out.

2 Brush rubber cement onto the back of each shape and adhere the shapes to poster board; let dry. Trim around the shapes. Fold the nose sharply on the crease lines. Using the craft knife and cutting mat, make slits in the mask for the nose piece.

3 Brush rubber cement on the black mask and the features of the Mask Topper face. Sprinkle the wet rubber cement with black glitter; let dry.

4 Using a piercing tool, poke a small hole in both sides of the mask. Thread gold stretch cord through the holes and secure in place with a knot.

5 Slide the flaps of the nose piece through the slits and fold the nose back crisply to lock in place.

6 *To make the tassel:* Using desired color, cut two 4 x 36-inch (10.2 x 91.4 cm) crepe paper strips. To form the fringe, cut the ¼-inch (0.6 cm) strips along the 36-inch (91.4 cm) edge, leaving ½ inch (1.3 cm) uncut. Starting at the 4-inch (10.2 cm) edge, roll the crepe paper tightly, jelly-roll style. Wrap the uncut end with a piece of cellophane tape to keep the tassel tightly rolled. Fluff the tassel.

7 Brush rubber cement on the taped area and adhere the tassel to the tip of the hat, or the ear.

Materials

- Cardstock: white, 8½ x 10 inches (21.6 x 25.4 cm) (4)
- Cellophane tape
- Crepe paper: black, orange
- Glitter: black
- Poster board
- Rubber cement
- Stretch cord: gold (13 inches [33.0 cm])

Tools

- Computer and printer or color copier
- Craft knife
- Craft scissors
- Paintbrush: small
- Piercing tool

45

Party Picks

Two 1920s German lapel pins from my vintage Halloween collection were the inspiration for these party picks. Hand-sculpted paper clay heads adorn skewers and make a delightful addition to dessert or hors d'oeuvre trays.

Instructions

1   Shape the desired party pick head from polymer clay using your fingers. Using a wooden skewer, form the ridges, mouth shape, and eyes. The circumference of the head should be approximately 2½ inches (6.4 cm).

2   Cut the skewers to measure 4½ inches (11.4 cm) long. Insert one wooden skewer into the base of the sculpted head. Bake the clay pieces according to manufacturer's directions.

3   Allow the clay pieces to cool then paint them as desired using acrylic paints.

4   From both colors of crepe paper, cut one ½ x 6-inch (3.8 x 15.2 cm) strip. Cut ⅛-inch- (0.3 cm) long strips along one 6-inch (15.2 cm) side to form a fringe.

5   Hot glue the uncut edge of the fringed strip to the base of the party pick head with the fringe pointing toward the head; let dry. Fold the fringe down to form the collar.

Materials

- Acrylic paint: black, orange, red
- Crepe paper: black, orange
- Polymer clay
- Wooden skewers

Tools

- Craft scissors
- Hot glue gun and glue sticks
- Oven
- Paintbrush: size 000
- Ruler

Tips & Tricks

Baking is Optional

The party picks can be made with paper clay. Paper clay doesn't require any baking time as it air dries, and it can be painted and embellished as desired.

Chapter 3

The Stitching Hour

Appliqué is the technique of stitching one fabric to another. Our opulent wool appliquéd pillows and decorations will add an element of richness to your Halloween home. Early settlers in America used the appliqué technique on their home goods to turn plain, humble fabrics, such as wool, into beautiful works of art. Everyday items were made from snippets of a skirt, an old coat, or a favorite shawl.

The pillows shown here are still made the old-fashioned way, with hand-dyed wool and intricate hand-embroidered crazy quilt stitches. In our projects, we used the fern stitch, French knots, chain stitch, and lazy daisy stitch, to name a few. You may want to purchase a book on quilt embroidery or stitching techniques to learn a few more. Use embroidery scissors to cut out small shapes and trim threads.

As you work through these projects, remember that ripping out stitches is an essential part of doing needlework of almost any type. If you don't like the stitches you have made, it is better to re-do them or start over with a different stitch. However, a little unevenness can be more interesting on a folk-style pillow, so don't be too hard on yourself.

Trick-or-Treat Table Runner

Halloween is the perfect time to add a touch of whimsy to your home. This table runner features a scaredy cat and petrified pumpkin. Made from wool in a layered style and appliquéd using a blanket stitch, this runner is similar to penny rugs that were made in the United States during the Civil War. The layering technique adds color and dimension to any project. Remember that wool runners are for decorative use and not recommended for areas where food is served or eaten. They are dry clean only.

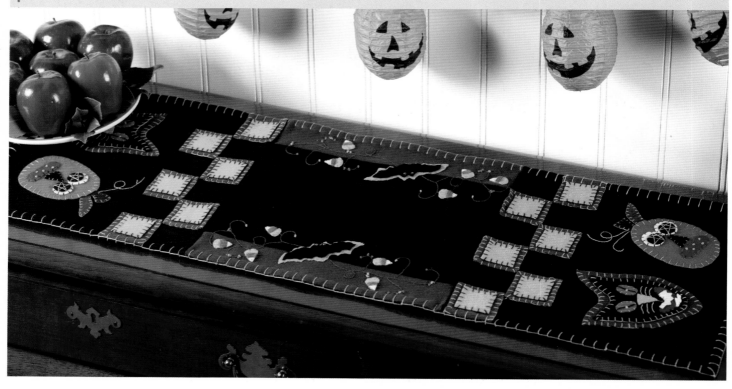

Instructions

Runner

1 From black wool, cut one 12¾ x 37-inch (32.4 x 94.0 cm) piece, one 12¾-inch (32.4 cm) square, and one 8½ x 13-inch (21.6 x 33.0 cm) piece. From dark green wool, cut two 3 x 13-inch (7.6 x 33.0 cm) pieces.

2 Starting at the seam on the top side of the runner, sew the green strips to the smallest black rectangle with ¼-inch (0.6 cm) seams. Sew the black squares on each end with a ½-inch (1.3 cm) seam. Do not attach the back panel.

Square Embellishments

1 Using the Large and Small Square templates (page 110), cut six large squares from purple wool and six small squares from gold wool.

2 Using three strands of black embroidery floss, sew the small gold squares on top of the large purple squares with a blanket stitch.

3 Using three strands of soft gold embroidery floss, appliqué the purple squares to the background in two rows of three with the top row along the seam, joining the end pieces to the middle piece with a blanket stitch.

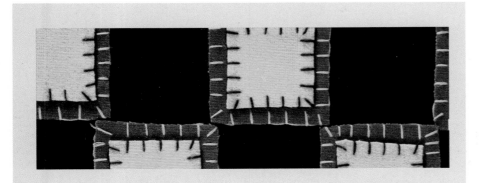

Materials

- Chenille needle: size 20
- Embroidery floss: black, dark orange, purple, soft gold
- Thread: black
- Wool: black—1½ yards (1.37 meters); brown—12-inch (30.5 cm) square; dark gold—½ yard (0.46 meter); dark green—½ yard (0.46 meter); dark red—12-inch (30.5 cm) square; gold—12-inch (30.5 cm) square; orange—12-inch (30.5 cm) square; purple—12-inch (30.5 cm) square; white—12-inch (30.5 cm) square

Tools

- Computer and printer or color copier
- Ruler
- Scissors: craft, embroidery
- Sewing machine

Cat Embellishments

1 Using the Cat Background template (page 109), cut one shape from dark green wool. Using the Cat Face template (page 109), cut one shape from black wool.

2 Using the Cat Eyes template (page 109), cut two shapes from dark gold wool. Using the Cat Nose template (page 109), cut one shape from gold wool. Using the Cat Mouth template (page 109), cut one mouth shape from dark red wool and one of each teeth shape from white wool.

3 Center the black cat face over the green cat background. Using three strands of soft gold embroidery floss, sew the pieces together with a blanket stitch.

4 Position the mouth and sew to the face with a backstitch using three strands of black embroidery floss.

5 Position the eyes and nose on the face and sew on with an appliqué stitch using three strands of soft gold embroidery floss. Add a French knot in the center of each eye.

6 Using three strands of soft gold embroidery floss, sew the finished cat face to the runner with a blanket stitch.

7 Using three strands of soft gold embroidery floss, form the whiskers with a couching stitch. Using three strands of black embroidery floss, form the lines through the eyes with a couching stitch.

8 Repeat steps 1–7 for the cat on the opposite end of the runner.

Pumpkin Embellishments

1 Using the Pumpkin template (page 109), cut one shape from orange wool. Using the Pumpkin Eyes template (page 109), cut two large shapes from white wool and two small shapes from brown wool.

2 Using the Pumpkin Nose template (page 109), cut one shape from black wool. Using the Pumpkin Mouth template (page 109), cut one shape from dark red wool.

3 Using the Pumpkin Stem template (page 109), cut one shape from brown wool. Using the Pumpkin Leaf template (page 109), cut one shape from dark green wool.

4 Using three strands of black embroidery floss, add white eye shapes to the pumpkin with appliqué stitching. Using three strands of soft gold embroidery floss, sew the brown eye shapes to the white eye shapes with stitches in the shape of a star.

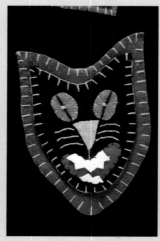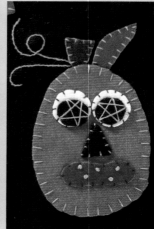

5 Using three strands of soft gold embroidery floss, sew the nose on the pumpkin with appliqué stitching. Using three strands of black embroidery floss, sew the mouth on the pumpkin with appliqué stitching. Using three strands of soft gold embroidery floss, add French knots to the mouth.

6 Position the pumpkin, stem, and leaf on the runner and sew on using three strands of soft gold embroidery floss and blanket stitching. Using two strands of soft gold embroidery floss, stitch the pumpkin vine with running stitches.

7 Repeat steps 1–6 for the pumpkin on the opposite side of the runner.

Bat Embellishments

1 Using the Bat Background template (page 110), cut one shape from gold wool. Using the Bat Body template (page 110), cut one shape from black wool.

2 Using three strands of soft gold embroidery floss, sew the bat background to the runner with appliqué stitching.

3 Using black embroidery floss, sew the bat body to the bat background using appliqué stitching.

4 Using two strands of soft gold embroidery floss, sew the eyes to the bat face.

5 Repeat steps 1–4 for the bats on the opposite side of the runner.

Candy Corn Embellishments

1 Using the Candy Corn Base template (page 110), cut five shapes from gold wool. Using the Candy Corn Tip template (page 110), cut five shapes from white wool.

2 Layer the white shapes on the gold shapes and sew to the runner using three strands of soft gold embroidery floss with appliqué stitching. Using three strands of dark orange embroidery floss, embellish each layered shape with satin stitching around the center of the shapes.

3 Using three strands of purple embroidery floss, create the vine with running stitches. Add French knots using dark orange and gold embroidery floss.

4 Repeat steps 1–3 for the candy corn on the opposite side of the runner.

To Finish the Runner

1 Place the right side of the front and back runner pieces together and machine stitch with ¼-inch (0.6 cm) seam. Make sure to leave an open area to turn the piece right side out.

2 Turn the runner right side out and blanket stitch around the edges using six strands of soft gold embroidery floss.

Crazy Quilt Pumpkin Pillow

Beautiful embroidery and hand stitching make this pillow a true piece of history. It features a log cabin block border and embroidery techniques that have evolved over time. The combination of deep fall foliage colors lends richness and charm. Spider webs and spiders are two of the most-often-used symbols appearing on early Victorian needlework quilts or pillows. Today, they provide an ideal Halloween background.

Instructions

To Form the Quilt Square Pillow Top

Machine stitch a ¼-inch (0.6 cm) seam attaching the strips in the following order, beginning with the left side of the black square: orange, rust, gold, orange-and-black plaid, light green, purple-and-black plaid, purple, and dark green. *Note:* You will be progressing in a clockwise fashion.

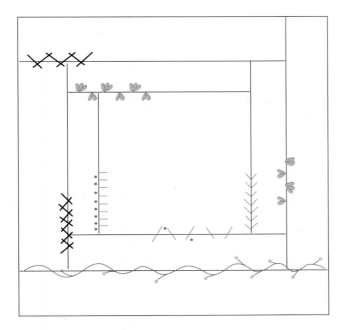

To Make and Attach the Pumpkin to the Pillow Top

1 Using the Pillow Pumpkin template (page 108), cut one pumpkin from orange wool. Using the Pillow Pumpkin Eyes template (page 108), cut two shapes from rust wool. Using the Pillow Pumpkin Nose template (page 108), cut one shape from red wool. Using the Pillow Pumpkin Teeth template (page 108), cut one shape from white wool.

Materials

- Beads: large black (4); small black iridescent (11); small white pearl (approximately 130)
- Chenille needle: size 20
- Embroidery floss: black, burnt orange, dark red, ecru, gold, light green
- Graphite paper
- Polyester fiber fill
- Thread: black
- Wool: black—6½-inch (16.5 cm) square; 12-inch (30.5 cm) square; plus 3-inch (7.6 cm) square for spider; dark green—2½ x 13½-inch (6.4 x 34.3 cm) piece plus small piece for leaf; gold—2 x 8-inch (5.1 x 20.3 cm) piece; light green—2½ x 9½-inch (6.4 x 24.2 cm) piece plus small piece for stem; orange—2 x 6½-inch (5.1 x 16.5 cm) piece plus small piece for pumpkin; orange-and-black plaid—2 x 9½-inch (5.1 x 24.2 cm) piece; purple—2½ x 11½-inch (6.4 x 29.2 cm) piece; purple-and-black plaid—2½ x 11½-inch (6.4 x 29.2 cm) piece; red—small scrap; rust—2 x 8-inch (5.1 x 20.3 cm) piece plus small piece for eyes; white—3-inch (7.6 cm) square

Tools

- Computer and printer or color copier
- Ruler
- Scissors: craft, embroidery
- Sewing machine

2 Using the Pillow Pumpkin Stem template (page 108), cut one shape from light green wool. Using the Pillow Pumpkin Leaf template (page 108), cut one shape from dark green wool.

3 Using one strand of black embroidery floss, attach two large black beads to the eyes. Using two strands of black embroidery floss, sew the eyes and nose to the pumpkin face with a backstitch.

4 Using two strands of dark red embroidery floss, stitch the teeth on the white mouth with a backstitch. Using two strands of ecru embroidery floss, appliqué the mouth to the pumpkin with a backstitch.

5 Using the project photograph for reference, position the pumpkin on the pillow top. Using two strands of black embroidery floss, appliqué the pumpkin to the pillow top with a blanket stitch. *Note:* The stitches shown are ¼ inch (0.6 cm) long.

6 Using two strands of light green embroidery floss, stitch the vein on the leaf with a backstitch then appliqué the leaf to the pillow top using a backstitch.

7 Using two strands of black embroidery floss, appliqué the light green stem to the top of the pumpkin with a backstitch.

To Stitch Vines Around Pumpkin

Using two strands of light green embroidery floss, sew the vines with a backstitch. Using gold embroidery floss, add French knots to the vines.

To Sew Border Stitches

1 Using three strands of burnt orange embroidery floss, sew a fern stitch on the border of the black center square and rust wool.

2 Using three strands of gold embroidery floss, sew a lazy daisy stitch in loops of two and three along the borders of the rust and black wool and gold and purple wool. *Note:* The stitches shown are ¼ inch (0.6 cm) long with the center three stitches slightly longer.

3 Using four strands of light green embroidery floss, sew a chain stitch along the bottom of the pillow top to create a vine. Using two strands of dark red embroidery floss, add French knots to the ends of the light green vine.

4 Using two strands of dark red embroidery floss, straight stitch along the top of the bottom border and the left side of the black center square. Randomly add 40–45 long and short stitches and 40–45 French knots.

5 Using three strands of black embroidery floss, add a herringbone stitch on the right side border of the light green strip and the bottom border of the black-and-purple plaid strip. *Note:* The stitches shown are ½ inch (1.3 cm) long.

To Make and Attach Spider Web and Spider

1 Using the Pillow Spider Web template (page 109) and graphite paper, trace the design onto the pillow. Using one strand of ecru embroidery floss, sew the web design using a chain stitch. Add the small white pearl beads along the web.

2 Using the Pillow Spider Body template (page 109), cut the spider from black wool. Using one strand of black embroidery floss, sew the small black iridescent beads in a cluster on the spider's back, then sew two large black beads on the head for eyes.

3 Position the spider as shown. Using two strands of black embroidery floss, appliqué the spider onto the web with a backstitch. Using two strands of black embroidery floss, chain stitch eight legs onto the spider.

To Form the Pillow

1 Place the right sides of the pillow top and the 12-inch (30.5 cm) black wool square together and machine stitch using a ¼-inch (0.6 cm) seam. Leave an opening at the bottom of the pillow for turning and stuffing.

2 Turn right side out and stuff the pillow with polyester fiber fill. Hand sew the opening closed with black thread.

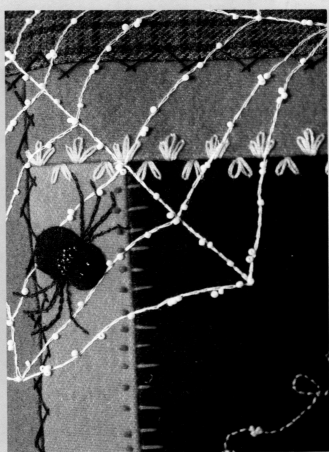

Flying Bats Beware!

Bats are mysterious animals of the night, but these three creatures won't give you a fright. Go batty with these bewitching flying bats. Give an eerie twist to your chandelier or hang them from a doorknob. For those of you venturing into embroidery and appliqué for the first time, these are great beginner projects.

Pumpkin Patch Bat

Instructions

To Make the Pumpkin Patch Bat

1. Using the Pumpkin Patch Bat template (page 110), cut two shapes from black wool. One shape is the front of the bat. Set the second shape aside; this is the back of the bat and will not be embellished.

2. Using the Bat Eyes template (page 112), cut two shapes from white wool. Using the Bat Nose template (page 112), cut one shape from red wool. Using the Bat Teeth template (page 112), cut one shape from white wool.

3 Using the Large and Small Leaves templates (page 112), cut two shapes of each from green wool. Using the Large Pumpkin template (page 112), cut one shape from orange wool. Using the Small Pumpkin template (page 112), cut two shapes from orange wool.

4 Using two strands of black embroidery floss, sew the large beads to the white eyes, and then sew the eyes to the bat face. *Note:* There is no stitching around the edges of the eyes.

5 Using two strands of black embroidery floss, appliqué the nose and teeth to the bat face.

6 Using two strands of green embroidery floss, sew the pumpkins to the bat with blanket stitching. *Note:* The largest pumpkin is in the center and the two smaller pumpkins are slightly under the large pumpkin.

7 Using two strands of green embroidery floss, sew ridges on the pumpkins using backstitching.

8 Using two strands of green embroidery floss, sew the leaves to the stems with blanket stitching. Using two strands of green embroidery floss, sew veins on the leaves with backstitching.

9 Using three strands of green embroidery floss, create vines using backstitching. Using six strands of dark red embroidery floss, add French knots to the ends of the vines.

To Finish the Pumpkin Patch Bat

1 Place the wrong sides of the bat together. Using six strands of dark orange embroidery floss, blanket stitch around the edges of the bat. *Note:* The stitches are approximately ¼ inch (0.6 cm) long. Leave a 3½-inch (8.9 cm) opening near the bottom, but don't cut the embroidery floss.

2 Stuff the bat with batting. Pick up the needle and continue blanket stitching to close.

To Make the Hanger

Crochet the hanger using black cotton crochet thread. Begin and end the hanger with a backstitch to the bat's head. *Note:* Our hanger is 22 inches (55.9 cm) long.

Spider Web Bat

Materials

- Batting
- Beads: large black (2); large iridescent black (1); small iridescent (2)
- Embroidery floss: black, dark orange, ecru
- Graphite paper: white
- Thread: black cotton crochet size 91
- Wool: black—7 x 12-inch (17.8 x 30.5 cm) piece (2); red, white—small remnant of each

Tools

- Chenille needle: size 20
- Computer and printer or color copier
- Crochet needle
- Pencil
- Ruler
- Scissors: craft, embroidery

Instructions

To Make Spider Web Bat

1 Using the Spider Web Bat template (page 111), cut two shapes from black wool. One shape is the front of the bat. Set the second shape aside—this is the back of the bat and will not be embellished.

2 Using the Bat Eyes template (page 112), cut two shapes from the white wool. Using the Bat Nose template (page 112), cut one shape from the red wool. Using the Bat Teeth template (page 112), cut one shape from the white wool.

3 Using two strands of black embroidery floss, sew the large black beads to the white eyes, and then sew the eyes to the bat face. *Note:* There is no stitching around the edges of the eyes.

4 Using two strands of black embroidery floss, appliqué the nose and teeth to the bat face.

5 Using the Web template (page 111), trace the pattern onto the bat using graphite paper. Using one strand of ecru embroidery floss, chain stitch the web shape onto the bat. Stitch the large and small iridescent beads on the web using two strands of ecru embroidery floss.

6 Using three strands of ecru embroidery floss, add wing "veins" on the bat with fern stitching. *Note:* The veins are slightly curved with the ones near the tip of the wing curved the most. The length of the longest vein is 2½ inches (6.4 cm) and the one nearest the spider web is 1½ inches (3.8 cm). The individual herringbone stitches are ¾ inch (0.9 cm) long.

To Finish the Spider Web Bat

1 Place the wrong sides of the bat together. Using six strands of dark orange embroidery floss, blanket stitch around the edges of the bat; don't cut the floss. The stitches are approximately ¼ inch (0.6 cm) long. Leave a 3½-inch (8.9 cm) opening near the bottom.

2 Stuff the bat with batting. Pick up the needle and continue blanket stitching to close.

To Make the Hanger

Crochet the hanger using black cotton crochet thread. Begin and end the hanger with a backstitch to the bat's head. Our hanger is 22 inches (55.9 cm) long.

Pumpkin Vines Bat

Instructions

To Make the Pumpkin Vines Bat

1 Using the Pumpkin Vines Bat template (page 111), cut two shapes from black wool. One shape is the front of the bat. Set the second shape aside—this is the back of the bat and will not be embellished.

2 Using the Bat Eyes template (page 112), cut two shapes from white wool. Using the Bat Nose template (page 112), cut one shape from red wool Using the Bat Teeth template (page 112), cut one shape from white wool. Using the Large and Small Leaves templates (page 112), cut 30 shapes from dark green wool.

3 Using two strands of black embroidery floss, sew the large beads onto the white eyes, and then sew the eyes to the bat face. *Note:* There is no stitching around the edges of the eyes.

4 Using two strands of black embroidery floss, appliqué the nose and teeth to the bat face.

5 Using two strands of green embroidery floss, create eight vines with backstitching. *Note:* Lengths vary as do the curves on the vines.

6 Using two strands of green embroidery floss, appliqué the leaves on the vines. Using six strands of dark orange embroidery floss, add French knots on the vines.

7 Using two strands of embroidery floss, backstitch desired word on the bat.

To Finish the Pumpkin Vines Bat

1 Place the wrong sides of the bat together. Using six strands of dark orange embroidery floss, blanket stitch around the edges of the bat; don't cut the floss. *Note:* The stitches are approximately ¼ inch (0.6 cm) long. Leave a 3½-inch (8.9 cm) opening near the bottom.

2 Stuff the bat with batting. Pick up the needle and continue blanket stitching to close.

To Make the Hanger

Crochet the hanger using black cotton crochet thread. Begin and end the hanger with a backstitch to the bat's head. Our hanger is 22 inches (55.9 cm) long.

Materials

- Batting
- Beads: large black (2)
- Embroidery floss: black, dark orange, green
- Thread: black cotton crochet size 91
- Wool: black—7 x 14-inch (17.8 x 35.6 cm) piece (2); dark green, red, white—small remnant of each

Tools

- Chenille needle: size 20
- Computer and printer or color copier
- Crochet needle
- Ruler
- Scissors: craft, embroidery

Door Hangers

Adorn your doorknobs or add these little pillows to a Halloween vignette on a shelf or side table. You can also fill them with potpourri for a touch of fall fragrance. Their harvest moon and window light will cast a ghostly spell on all who enter.

Frightfully Fun Feline

Materials

- Beads: small amber (2); small white (1)
- Embroidery floss: black, ecru
- Polyester fiber fill
- Ribbon: black-and-white polka dot (12 inches [30.5 cm])
- Thread: black
- Wool: black—7 x 9-inch (17.8 x 22.9 cm) pieces (2) plus 6-inch (15.2 cm) square; gold—4½ x 6¼-inch (11.4 x 15.8 cm) piece; white—5 x 7-inch (12.7 x 17.8 cm) piece

Tools

- Computer and printer or color copier
- Needles: chenille size 20, sewing
- Ruler
- Scissors: craft, embroidery
- Sewing machine

Instructions

To Make the Frightfully Fun Feline Door Hanger

1 Using the Moon template (page 112), cut one shape from gold wool. Using the Cat template (page 112), cut one shape from black wool. Using the Fence template (page 112), cut one shape from white wool.

2 Using three strands of ecru embroidery floss, sew the moon to 7 x 9-inch (17.8 x 22.9 cm) piece of black wool. *Note:* This is the pillow top. Our stitches are ¼ inch (0.6 cm) long. The moon is 1¼ inches (3.2 cm) from the top and is centered on its sides.

3 Using two strands of black embroidery floss, sew the cat to the moon with blanket stitching, making sure to center the cat on the moon. Sew on amber beads for the eyes and a white bead for the nose. Using two strands of ecru embroidery floss, chain stitch three whiskers on each side of the cat's face.

4 Position the fence on the pillow top overlapping the moon and cat's paws. (The bottom edge of the fence is 1¼ inches [3.2 cm] from the edge of the pillow.) Using two strands of black embroidery floss, sew the fence to the pillow top using blanket stitching.

To Finish the Frightfully Fun Feline Door Hanger

1 Place the right sides of two 7 x 9-inch (17.8 x 22.9 cm) pieces of black wool together and machine stitch together with a ¼-inch (0.6 cm) seam. Leave an opening at the bottom for turning and stuffing.

2 Turn right side out and stuff the pillow with polyester fiber fill. Hand sew the opening closed with black thread.

3 Using six strands of ecru thread, blanket stitch the edges of the pillow. Our blanket stitch is ⅜ inch (0.9 cm) long.

4 Cut two 6-inch (15.2 cm) pieces of ribbon. Stitch one piece on each top corner of the pillow. Tie the ribbons together at the top to form a bow.

Ghoulish Ghost

Instructions

To Make the Ghoulish Ghost Door Hanger

1 Using the Window template (page 113), cut one shape from gold wool.

2 Cut one ¾ x 1¼-inch (1.9 x 3.2 cm) piece of black wool.

3 Cut two ¼ x 4½-inch (0.6 x 11.4 cm) strips and two ¼ x 6½-inch (0.6 x 16.5 cm) strips from black wool.

4 Using the Ghost template (page 113), cut one shape from white wool, and then cut out the mouth and eyes. Attach ¾ x 1¼-inch (1.9 x 3.2 cm) piece of black wool behind the open mouth and eyes of the ghost by overhand stitching around each opening using one strand of ecru embroidery floss.

5 Using two strands of black embroidery floss, stitch the black strips to the window shape using an overhand stitch.

6 Using three strands of ecru embroidery floss, sew the window to one 7 x 9-inch (17.8 x 22.9 cm) piece of black wool with blanket stitching. *Note:* Our blanket stitches are ¼ inch (0.6 cm) wide.

7 Using two strands of ecru embroidery floss, sew the ghost to the window with blanket stitching.

To Finish the Ghoulish Ghost Door Hanger

1 Place the right sides of two 7 x 9-inch (17.8 x 22.9 cm) pieces of black wool together and machine stitch with a ¼-inch (0.6 cm) seam. Leave an opening at the bottom for turning and stuffing.

2 Cut two 6-inch (15.2 cm) pieces of ribbon. Stitch one piece on each top corner of the pillow. Tie the ribbons together at the top to form a bow.

3 Turn right side out and stuff the pillow with polyester fiber fill. Hand sew the opening closed with black thread.

4 Using six strands of ecru embroidery floss, blanket stitch around the edges of the pillow. *Note:* Our blanket stitches are ⅜ inch (0.9 cm) wide.

Materials

- Embroidery floss: black, ecru
- Polyester fiber fill
- Ribbon: black-and-white polka dot (12 inches [30.5 cm])
- Thread: black
- Wool: black—7 x 9-inch (17.8 x 22.9 cm) pieces (2) plus 6-inch (15.2 cm) square; gold—6 x 8-inch (15.2 x 20.3 cm) piece; white—4-inch (10.2 cm) square

Tools

- Computer and printer or color copier
- Needles: chenille size 20, sewing
- Ruler
- Scissors: craft, embroidery
- Sewing machine

Chapter 4

Tricks and Treats
for Little Goblins

October 31st is a night that children anticipate with keen delight. It casts a spell on children of all ages— an evening of fantasy and imagination. When planning a children's Halloween party, keep it fun and entertaining. Anything that frightens should be avoided.

Even without ghosts and skeletons, darkness and wild noises, there is still much to fascinate and furnish an exciting time. Smiling jack-o-lanterns and silly skeletons are sure to set a happy mood.

Children love to play games and eat lots of goodies. They also love to make things, so don't hesitate to include them when creating party decor and favors. This chapter features projects to create a fun, child-friendly celebration.

Let's Party Invites

Small children love to receive party invitations by mail. By using a vintage postcard image featuring Halloween children, you can create a special greeting that will excite and delight little guests. Make them colorful and fun, using symbols in place of words for the important "who, when, and where" of the party. This invitation includes a blank piece of paper for the recipient's Halloween artwork as the RSVP.

Instructions

1. Copy the Polka Dot Paper (page 118), Child's Vintage image (page 114), and Let's Party images (page 113) onto cardstock. Trim the paper and images to fit the invitation.

2. Using the paintbrush, apply rubber cement to the back of the Polka Dot Paper and adhere it to the front of the invitation. Apply rubber cement to the back of the Child's Vintage image and adhere it to the inside of the invitation. Apply rubber cement to the back of the Let's Party images and adhere them to the left inside flap.

3. Using a gel pen, fill in the specific time, place, date, and host/hostess information. Embellish the front of the invitation with Halloween-themed stickers.

4. Enclose a blank 4½ x 5½-inch (11.4 x 14 cm) piece of cardstock in the invitation along with a handwritten note asking the recipient to color a Halloween image on the cardstock, and then return it as the RSVP. Ask them to print their name by the picture. *Note:* These drawings can be used to create the Little Goblins Treat Bags (page 72).

Materials

- Cardstock: white, 8½ x 10 inches (21.6 x 25.4 cm)
- Halloween-themed stickers
- Pre-made invitation: black
- Rubber cement
- Vellum envelope: white

Tools

- Computer and printer or color copier
- Craft scissors
- Gel pen
- Paintbrush: small
- Pencil
- Ruler

Little Goblins Treat Bags

The expression "trick-or-treat" became the Halloween greeting during the late 1930s or early 1940s. This mini treat bag is made as a party favor from the little goblin guests' artwork that was returned as the Let's Party Invite RSVP. Children will be proud to show off their very own creation as they gobble their goodies.

Instructions

1 Have each child color a Halloween picture, or use the pictures returned as the RSVP from the Let's Party Invite (page 70). *Note:* Make sure the drawing is the correct size to fit your treat bags.

2 Follow manufacturer's directions to copy and make iron-on transfers of the child's drawing onto the canvas bag.

3 Cut desired lengths of ribbon, and then hot glue the ribbon to the handles of the canvas bag. Add paper grass and treats as desired.

Materials

- Canvas bag: small
- Halloween drawing
- Iron-on transfer paper
- Paper grass
- Ribbon
- Treats

Tools

- Craft scissors
- Hot glue gun and glue sticks
- Iron

Tips & Tricks

Trick-or-Treat Bags

Employ the same technique to make a larger canvas bag for your little ones to use when trick or treating. Personalize the bag with images of your little goblins. Embellish the bag with buttons, ribbon, or feathers. What a memorable night it will be!

Crepe Paper Party Hats

None of us ever outgrow the pleasure of "dressing up," so give your guests a cap to don. These crepe paper party hats are recreations of 1930s German party hats. Crepe paper hats became generally popular beginning in 1912 when craft books that showed easy-to-make Halloween ideas for hats, costumes, and decorating were published. Since these hats were fragile and disposable, not many exist today, making them a favorite of collectors.

Instructions

To Make the Hat Band

1. Cut one strip of cardstock measuring 1 inch (2.5 cm) wide and the circumference of the head size you want the hat to fit. Add 1 inch (2.5 cm) to allow for overlap. *Note:* You may need to piece strips together to reach desired length.

2. Cut a strip of crepe paper on the bias (to keep it from stretching) of the color you wish for your hat band.

3. Using the paintbrush, spread rubber cement on one side of the cardstock strip and apply it to the crepe paper strip. Press firmly; let dry.

To Make the Hat Body

1. Cut a piece of crepe paper as long as your hat band and 8½ inches (21.6 cm) tall.

2. Using the paintbrush, spread rubber cement on the back of the hat band. *Note:* Put rubber cement only on the top ½ inch (1.3 cm) of the strip.

Materials

- Cardstock: white, 8½ x 11 inches (21.6 x 27.9 cm)
- Cellophane tape
- Crepe paper: black, cream, orange
- Rubber cement

Tools

- Computer and printer or color copier
- Craft scissors
- Paintbrush: small
- Pencil
- Ruler

3 Place a large sheet of crepe paper on the rubber cement and press gently; let dry. Using the paintbrush, spread rubber cement carefully on one end of the band and on one end of the crepe paper. Bring the two ends together, overlapping about 1 inch (2.5 cm). *Note:* We glued the band first and placed a paper clamp to hold the ends together.

4 Gently bring the edges of the crepe paper hat body together (this will form a cylinder shape); let dry.

To Shape the Hat

1 Crease the sides of the hat. Do not pull the crepe paper. *Note:* The glued seam is the center front of the hat.

2 Fold the right corner to make a seam. Fold the left corner to make a seam, overlapping to form another ¼-inch (0.6 cm) seam. Adjust as needed to form a nice point on the tip of the hat. Glue the seam together with rubber cement.

To Embellish the Hat

1 Cut one 4 x 18-inch (10.2 x 45.7 cm) strip of crepe paper. Cut a 3-inch (7.6 cm) fringe along the 18-inch (45.7 cm) side of the strip.

2 Fold the strip to make a tassel and wrap the tassel with cellophane tape. *Note:* Our tassel is 1½ inches (3.8 cm) wide at the top. The tassel needs to be flat as you will adhere an image to cover the tape.

3 Using the paintbrush, apply rubber cement to the base of the folded triangle on the top of the hat.

4 Copy the Cat, Pumpkin, and Skeleton Crepe Paper Hat images (page 114) onto cardstock; cut out. Using the paintbrush, apply rubber cement to the back of each image and adhere to the cellophane tape on the tassel.

Party Boy Pumpkin Picks

These pumpkin picks add sparkle to any Halloween decoration. Add a cluster to the center of your favorite dessert or to take-home treat bags.

Materials

- Cardstock: white, 8½ x 10 inches (21.6 x 25.4 cm)
- Cotton balls (6)
- Glitter: orange
- Rubber cement
- Spray paint: black
- Wooden skewers

Tools

- Computer and printer or color copier
- Craft scissors
- Paintbrush: small
- Ruler

Instructions

1   Copy the Party Boy Pumpkin images (page 115) onto cardstock. Cut out shapes.

2   Cut the skewers to measure 6 inches (15.2 cm) long. Spray paint each skewer; let dry.

3   Using a paintbrush, apply rubber cement to the back of two images, add a small bit of cotton between the images, and press the images together. *Note:* You don't need much cotton, just enough to slightly puff out the pumpkins.

4   Using the paintbrush, apply a light coat of rubber cement to the face of pumpkin, omitting the black areas. Sprinkle glitter on the wet rubber cement; let dry.

Pennant Garland

This pennant garland was inspired by a vintage collegiate-style pennant that my father had from his college days. Done up all sparkly in orange and black, this garland looks great swagged across a doorway, window, or above a treat table.

Instructions

1 Using the Pennant template (page 116), cut 16 shapes from matboard using a craft knife and cutting mat. Spray one side of each pennant with black paint; let dry. Spray black side of pennant with spray adhesive and sprinkle with black glitter.

2 Copy the Polka Dot Paper (page 118) and Pennant Garland images (page 117) onto cardstock. Cut the paper to fit the pennants. Adhere the paper to the pennants with adhesive spray. Adhere the images to the paper with adhesive spray.

3 Working one pennant at a time, spray adhesive on the blank side of each pennant and attach to the back of a colored, decorated pennant; let dry.

4 Working one pennant at a time, drizzle a thin line of hot glue around the edge of each pennant. Adhere black tinsel garland to the edges; trim with scissors. Using the awl, pierce each pennant with a tiny hole ½ inch (1.3 cm) in and down from the top corners.

5 Thread 3 inches (7.6 cm) of craft wire through each hole and attach the pennants to a long strand of tinsel garland. Tuck the ends of the wire into the garland. *Note:* The length of the tinsel garland strand will depend on the area in which it will be strung. Measure and cut as needed.

Materials

- Adhesive spray
- Cardstock: white, 8½ x 10 inches (21.6 x 25.4 cm)
- Craft wire: 26-gauge
- Glitter: black
- Matboard
- Spray paint: black
- Tinsel garland: black, orange

Tools

- Awl
- Computer and printer or color copier
- Craft knife
- Craft scissors
- Cutting mat
- Hot glue gun and glue sticks
- Ruler

Tips & Tricks

Hanging the Garland

To space your pennants on the orange tinsel garland, find the center of the strand and attach pennants from the center to the ends. Leave about 2½ feet (0.76 meters) of tinsel unadorned on each end for easy hanging.

The Halloween Queen Hat

A witch is usually portrayed as a hag-like woman with a pointy chin, nose, and hat, flying on a broomstick. For this stunning centerpiece I chose an atypical beautiful witch. The images featured on this project are of the Schmucker Girl from the Winsch Publishing Company printed in 1912. Because of the feminine nature of these images, I added ruffles of netting and flounces of festooning to create a classic focal point for a party table.

Instructions

1 Spray the papier-mâché hat inside and out with black paint; let dry completely.

2 Cut one 5 x 36-inch (12.7 x 91.4 cm) strip of ivory tulle. Sew a basting stitch lengthwise down the middle of the strip, and pull on the threads to gather. Adjust the gathers to the ruffle so it fits around the base of the hat. Apply hot glue along the edge of the hat where the rim meets the cone; press the gathered tulle into place.

3 Cut one 4 x 36-inch (10.2 x 91.4 cm) strip of orange tulle. Sew a basting stitch lengthwise down the middle of the strip, and pull on the threads to gather. Adjust the gathers to fit ruffle atop the ivory tulle, and then hot glue the orange tulle in place.

4 Cut one 3½ x 36-inch (8.9 x 91.4 cm) strip of black tulle. Sew a basting stitch lengthwise down the middle of the strip, and pull on the threads to gather. Adjust the gathers to fit ruffle atop the orange tulle, and then hot glue the black tulle into place.

5 From black, ivory, and orange tulle, cut one 3 x 14-inch (7.6 x 35.6 cm) strip of each color. Sew a basting stitch lengthwise down the middle of the strip, and pull on the threads to gather. Adjust the gathers to fit around the point of the hat, then hot glue the tulle pieces into place.

6 Cut one 3-inch (7.6 cm) strip of tissue paper garland. Hot glue the strip over the tulle gathers at the point of the hat.

7 Cut one 16-inch (40.6 cm) strip of tissue paper garland. Hot glue the strip over the tulle gathers around the base of the hat.

8 Copy the Queen images (page 119) onto cardstock and cut out with pinking shears. Brush the edges and small details on the images with craft glue and sprinkle with desired colors of glitter; let dry.

9 Adhere the images to the front and back of the hat using the small paintbrush and rubber cement.

Materials

- Cardstock: lightweight white, 8½ x 10 inches (21.6 x 25.4 cm)
- Craft glue
- Glitter: fine black, gold, iridescent white
- Papier-mâché witch hat: 13 x 16 inches (33.0 x 40.6 cm)
- Rubber cement
- Spray paint: black
- Thread: black
- Tissue paper garland
- Tulle: black, ivory, orange

Tools

- Computer and printer or color copier
- Craft scissors
- Hot glue gun and glue sticks
- Paintbrush: small
- Pinking shears
- Ruler
- Sewing machine

Chapter 5

Haunted Lights and Spooky Sights

The ingredients for a great Halloween party include a group of fun-loving kids and adults gathering together to share in good old-fashioned tomfoolery. And the best way to set the mood is to decorate so that an air of mystery pervades the gathering place.

In this chapter you will find ghostly luminaries along with witches, goblins, spiders, and bats to help you set the party atmosphere. Most any room in your house will provide a perfect party backdrop, from the kitchen to the living room to the dining room. If you don't have a large table to devote to the party setting, a buffet table is always an option.

Now, let the party begin…read horoscopes, tell ghost stories, and have a "monster mash." Fantasy and fun are the essence of every Halloween celebration, so for one mystical evening anything goes.

Ghoulish Glow Luminaries

My daughter, Erin, created luminaries from photographs to personalize her wedding tables. As soon as I saw them I imagined lanterns aglow with the shadows of vintage images.

I created these luminaries using vintage postcard images and early Halloween photographs from my friend Bruce. To personalize them, consider using pictures of your own little goblins to cast a ghoulish glow with these haunting lights. Stand the frames around a candle in a protective glass holder or spread them out across a table to create a ghostly scene.

Instructions

1 Spray picture mats with desired paint colors; let dry. Copy the Postcard Luminary (page 120), Silhouette Luminary (page 115), and Vintage Luminary (page 120) images onto vellum and trim to size, leaving an edge for placement of rubber cement.

2 Apply rubber cement to the back inside edges of the picture mats. Press trimmed vellum images over the opening.

3 Measure and cut ribbons to wrap around to the back of the mats. Secure the ribbons to the mats with double-sided tape.

4 Using cellophane tape, hinge the frames together so the three frames can be folded to form a triangle. *Note:* Cellophane tape works best as it cannot be seen along the edges of the mats.

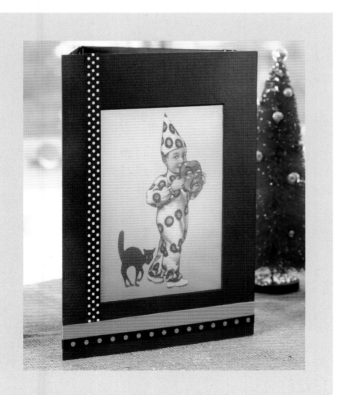

Materials

- Picture frame mats: white, 5 x 7 inch (12.7 x 17.8 cm) or 8 x 10 inch (20.3 x 25.4 cm) (3)
- Ribbon
- Rubber cement
- Spray paint: black, orange
- Tape: cellophane, double-sided
- Vellum: ivory, 8½ x 10 inches (21.6 x 25.4 cm) (9 sheets)

Tools

- Computer and printer or color copier
- Craft scissors
- Ruler

Tips & Tricks

Safety Reminders

To glow safely, always place candles in votive holders prior to using with the luminaries. You can also use battery-operated lights.

Papier-Mâché Masquerade

These Halloween character papier-mâché masks were originally created for a jack-o-lantern to wear, but they make perfect "people" masks too. Historically, this style of mask was popular at masquerade balls in Europe during the late 1800s and early 1900s. They are easy to make and very comfortable to wear. Anyone hesitant about wearing a full costume can hide behind one of these whimsical masks.

Instructions

1 Enlarge the eyes of the half mask using craft scissors. Cover the entire mask with masking tape (this gives the clay a good surface to grab onto).

2 Cut out, freehand-style, features such as ears, nose, hat, etc. from lightweight cardboard and adhere to the mask with masking tape.

3 Cover the masking tape and cardboard with paper clay. Smooth and shape the paper clay as desired; let dry.

4 Paint the mask as desired; let dry. *Note:* This is the fun part. Let your imagination run wild—emphasize the eyes with eyebrows and eyelashes, paint whiskers on a cat face, or paint a witch's face green.

5 Embellish the mask as desired using glitter, feathers, paper grass, etc. Adhere embellishments with hot glue.

Materials

- Acrylic paint: assorted colors
- Cardboard
- Craft glue
- Glitter: assorted colors
- Half mask
- Masking tape
- Paper clay
- Paper grass

Tools

- Craft scissors
- Feathers
- Hot glue gun and glue sticks
- Paintbrushes: medium, small

Spooky Spiders
with Spider Napkin Ring

These spooky spider table accessories are sure to give your guests quite the fright! We used them for place card holders, to adorn napkin rings, and to crawl all over our party table. They're fun and easy to make—have them appear anywhere your guests are least expecting.

Instructions

To Make the Spider's Body

1 Shape three balls of polymer clay: one 1⅜ x 1 inch (3.5 x 2.5 cm); one ½ inch (1.3 cm); and one ¼ inch (0.6 cm). Insert a toothpick through the center of the balls to fasten them together—like a snowman. Break off any toothpick that is showing at the ends.

2 Break the ends off a separate toothpick to form two antennae and insert them at the top of the smallest ball.

3 Bake the spider body per manufacturer's instructions; let cool. After the spider body has cooled, spray with black paint; let dry.

4 Spray the spider body with adhesive and sprinkle with glitter. Set the spider body aside.

To Make the Spider's Legs

1 Cut two 7½-inch (19.1 cm) lengths of 20-gauge wire, four 5½-inch (14 cm) lengths, and two 3½-inch (8.9 cm) lengths. Wrap each set of same-sized wire pieces together with floral tape—when finished you will have four legs.

2 Line up the legs: 7½ inch (19.1 cm), then 5½ inch (14 cm), then 3½ inch (8.9 cm). Wire all four legs together in the middle with 24-gauge wire and shape the spider legs.

3 Place hot glue on the wrapped wire at the middle of the legs, and then press the leg section onto the bottom of the middle ball of the body. Paint the spider's legs as desired.

Materials

- Acrylic paint: black, orange
- Adhesive spray
- Craft wire: 20-gauge, 24-gauge
- Floral tape
- Glitter: black
- Polymer clay
- Spray paint: black
- Wooden toothpicks

Tools

- Craft scissors
- Hot glue gun and glue sticks
- Oven
- Paintbrush: small

Spider Napkin Ring

Materials

- Napkin ring: wooden or metal
- Ribbon: black, ½ inch (1.3 cm) wide (6 inches [15.2 cm])
- Spooky Spider (see instructions on page 89)

Tools

- Craft scissors
- Hot glue gun and glue sticks

Instructions

1 Refer to the instructions on page 89 to create the all-black Spooky Spider.

2 Wrap black ribbon tightly around the napkin ring and hot glue the end of the ribbon to secure. Hot glue the Spooky Spider to the napkin ring.

Going Batty Candlesticks

For a dark and eerie ambiance, these Going Batty Candlesticks will provide flickering candlelight and shadows for your trick-or-treat table. They also look great on a mantel.

Materials

- Adhesive spray
- Cardstock: black
- Chenille pipe cleaners: black (6)
- Craft glue
- Glitter: black
- Spray paint: black
- Taper candles (3)
- Wooden candlesticks (3)

Tools

- Computer and printer or color copier
- Craft scissors
- Pencil

Instructions

1 Spray the candlesticks with black paint; let dry. Spray the candlesticks with adhesive, and then sprinkle with glitter; let dry.

2 Using the Candlestick Bats template (page 121), make six cardstock bats. Spray paint the front of the bats; let dry. Spray paint the back of the bats; let dry. Apply craft glue to the back of the bats and adhere together, sandwiching the end of one pipe cleaner between.

3 Spray the bats with adhesive, and then sprinkle glitter onto the wet adhesive. Gently twist pipe cleaners around a pencil, and then remove the pencil. Hold the ends of the pipe cleaners on the base of a candle as you insert it in the candlestick.

Pumpkin and Cat Decorations

Chairs and stairs are two of my favorite areas to haunt for a party. If you have a stairway banister, use black tulle netting or a black feather garland to hang these pumpkin and cat decorations. Or use them to decorate the back of a dining room chair.

Instructions

1. Copy Happy Jack-O-Lantern and Scary Cat images (page 121) onto cardstock. Using the paintbrush and rubber cement, adhere the images to cardboard; let dry. Cut out the images.

2. Cut the chenille pipe cleaner in half. Fold one cut piece in half and fasten this loop on the back of one image with cloth tape.

3. From each color crepe paper, cut six ½ x 7-inch (1.3 x 17.8 cm) strips. Fasten the strips to the back of the images with cloth tape.

4. Using the paintbrush, apply rubber cement to all black areas on the images. Sprinkle the rubber cement with glitter; let dry.

Materials

- Cardboard: 8½ x 10 inches (21.6 x 25.4 cm)
- Cardstock: heavyweight white, 8½ x 10 inches (21.6 x 25.4 cm)
- Chenille pipe cleaner: black
- Cloth tape: black
- Crepe paper: black, orange
- Glitter: black
- Rubber cement

Tools

- Computer and printer or color copier
- Craft scissors
- Paintbrush: small
- Ruler

Gypsy, the Folk Art Witch

In the beginning, I created holiday folk-art figures that featured vintage buttons, antique fabrics, and handmade accessories. Although my early faces were made of canvas, today I hand sculpt my pieces from paper clay or polymer clay. This folk art witch's face is made in a simplistic manner using paper clay over a polystyrene foam base.

Though this is a bit of an advanced project that requires basic sculpting and sewing skills, beginners should not be intimidated because imperfect features and proportions only add to the charm of a piece of folk art.

Instructions

To Sew the Doll's Body

1 Using a computer and printer or color copier, print the Witch Leg, Witch Arm, and Witch Body templates (pages 122–123). Cut out the patterns.

2 Position and pin the body and arm patterns on a double layer of black cotton fabric—right sides together. Cut fabric so there are four each of the arms and legs, and two body shapes.

3 Sew on the lines of the pattern pieces using the smallest stitch on the machine. Tear away the pattern pieces.

4 Cut one 5 x 36-inch (12.7 x 91.4 cm) piece of black cotton fabric and one 10 x 36-inch (25.4 x 91.4 cm) piece of black-and-white striped fabric with the stripe running horizontally.

5 Sew the black cotton fabric to the black-and-white striped fabric along the 36-inch (91.4 cm) edge, leaving

Materials

- Acrylic paint: black, flesh-tone, off-white, olive green, red
- Antiquing glaze: brown, green
- Cardstock: white, 8½ x 10 inches (21.6 x 25.4 cm)
- Craft glue
- Crepe paper: black, ivory, orange
- Decoupage medium
- Elastic: ¼ inch wide (0.6 cm)
- Embellishments: antique buttons, glittery old brooch, vintage coin purse
- Fabric: black cotton—36 inches (91.4 cm) wide (½ yard [0.46 meter]); black velvet—½ yard (0.46 meter); black-and-white striped—36 inches (91.4 cm) wide (½ yard [0.46 meter]); gray-and-white striped—½ yard (0.46 meter)
- Glass bead: orange
- Glitter: black
- Lamb's wool or wool doll's hair sold by the yard in long braids: gray
- Paper clay (16 oz. [460 grams])
- Plastic spider
- Polyester fiber fill
- Polystyrene foam ball (2 inches [5.1 cm])
- Remnant of old wool blanket or black lace
- Spray sealer
- Thread: black, machine, sewing, upholstery
- Tinsel: silver
- Trim: black, rayon braid, rayon cording (12 inches [30.5 cm] of each); ivory lace, 1-inch (2.5 cm) wide (½ yard [0.46 meter])
- Upholstery thread
- Wooden book: 2–3 inches (5.1–7.6 cm) tall or a tiny vintage book
- Wooden dowel: ⅛ x 4 inches (0.3 x 10.2 cm)

Tools

- Computer and printer or color copier
- Craft scissors
- Hot glue gun and glue sticks
- Needle: doll-making
- Paintbrushes: various sizes including fine 5/0
- Sandpaper: fine-grain
- Sewing machine
- Straight pins

a ⅝-inch (1.6 cm) seam allowance. Fold this panel in half with right sides together, matching stripes and black fabric evenly. Pin the leg pattern to the fabric and cut out fabric for two legs. Sew on the lines of the pattern pieces, and then tear away the pieces.

6 Trim the excess fabric from the arms, legs, and body, leaving a ¼-inch (0.6 cm) seam allowance all around. Make a slit at the top of each leg for turning and stuffing. Turn and stuff the body, arms, and legs with polyester fiber fill.

7 To attach the legs to the hips, thread a long doll-making needle with upholstery thread, and then sew back and forth through the legs from hip to hip to secure (3 to 4 times works well).

8 Sew a gathering stitch along the top of arms. Gather the stitches, and then tack the arms to the shoulders by tucking the raw edge under and slip stitching all the way around the opening.

9 Hot glue the black rayon braid trim around the legs where the black fabric meets the stripe. *Note:* The doll body should be complete with openings left for the head and hands.

To Sew the Doll's Clothes

Gypsy's skirt is made from a vintage robe sleeve. The width of the sleeve is approximately 24 inches (61.0 cm). Use black velveteen fabric for the skirt if you don't have remnants of old clothes.

1 Cut one 10¾ x 11-inch (27.3 x 27.9 cm) piece of black velveteen. Fold fabric in half widthwise and sew together along the 10¾-inch (27.3 cm) edge, leaving a 1½-inch (3.8 cm) opening at the top of the seam. Gather the top edge of the skirt and use a running stitch to hold the gathers in place.

2 Cut one 1¾ x 9-inch (4.4 x 22.9 cm) piece of black velveteen fabric. Fold the fabric in half lengthwise with the right sides together. Sew across the ends, and then turn the waistband right side out. Pin the waistband to the skirt, adjusting the gathers. Match the waistband edges to the skirt opening edges and sew the pieces together.

3 Sew the ivory lace trim along the bottom edge of the skirt.

Gypsy's blouse is next. Her blouse was made from a vintage-looking robe lining. To create the blouse, use a gray-and-white striped cotton fabric.

1 Using the Witch Blouse template (page 124), cut two shapes from gray-and-white striped cotton fabric. Using a ¼-inch (0.6 cm) seam allowance, sew the blouse together at the shoulder seams. Open flat.

2 Using the Witch Blouse Sleeve template (page 125), cut two shapes from gray-and-white striped cotton fabric. Sew a gathering stitch along the sleeve caps. Gather the sleeve caps, pin, adjust the gathers, and then sew one sleeve to the left side of the Witch Blouse and one sleeve to the right side.

3 Fold up a ½-inch- (1.3 cm) hem for the elastic casing on the bottom of each sleeve, pin, and sew. Cut two 3¼-inch- (8.2 cm) long pieces of elastic. Insert one piece of elastic into the elastic casing on each sleeve, and stitch the ends of the elastic together.

4 With the right sides together, sew the side seams of the Witch Blouse and the sleeves together. Hem the Witch Blouse if desired.

5 Dress the doll before attaching the sculpted head and hands. Slipstitch the skirt and blouse in place where needed.

To Make the Doll's Head

For this doll, I used a very simplistic sculpting style with paper clay applied over a polystyrene foam ball. With some practice and experimentation, this is the easiest method for beginning sculptors. The paper clay will air dry and can be worked in layers. It can be sanded and smoothed with sandpaper after completion. Don't be afraid to move the clay around until you get a look you like. As you work on the face, take your time and continue smoothing the clay, making each area flow into the other. A funny, somewhat wacky face could be great on a witch, so don't aim for perfection. Let the sculpture dry 2 to 3 days.

1 Cover a 2-inch (5.1 cm) polystyrene foam ball with a thin, even layer of paper clay, smoothing it out until you have a clay ball. You can let the clay ball harden overnight or continue at this point.

2 In the upper center of the face, apply a small coil of clay to form the nose. Apply two more coils of clay above the nose on each side to form the ridge of the eyebrows. Smooth these coils into the face, creating a general shape.

Tips & Tricks

Working with Paper Clay
While sculpting the doll's head and hands, you will need to smooth the clay into place. Occasionally dipping your fingers in water will help in the smoothing process.

Drying Time
Because the paper clay pieces need to dry for 2 to 3 days, consider making them in one or two days, and then constructing the body and clothes during the days the clay pieces are drying.

3 Add two small balls of clay under the eyebrow ridge and push them into the face, smoothing out the paper clay to form the eye area (see fig. 1). The slight indented space will be where Gypsy's eyes are painted.

Forming the face

Fig. 1   Fig. 2   Fig. 3

4 Apply a ball of clay in the center of the face for the nose. Smooth and shape the nose as desired (see fig 2). *Note:* I make my witch's noses larger and somewhat hooked with a crooked look. The nose is narrow at the bridge and I sometimes add tiny little balls of clay to each side when forming the flared-out base of her nose. The end of a paint-brush works well to make tiny nostrils. I also like to add moles for a witchy look.

5 Apply a ball of clay to each side of her face to form cheekbones. Smooth and shape the cheek-bones as desired. Apply a small ball of clay to the bottom of her face to form the chin (see fig 3). *Note:* You can exaggerate the cheekbones or keep her face skinny and haggard—it's fun to play with this portion of the face to add character. I usually over-emphasize this area too and add a wart for good measure.

6 Add a coil of clay under the nose for the mouth and smooth it into the cheekbone area. *Note:* I find the mouth the most difficult feature to sculpt. The muscles of the upper lip always lay over the top of the bottom lip, so I form the upper lip first and then layer the lower lip. I press the clay into a slight indent on each side of the mouth to form her smirky smile. Using the end of my paintbrush, I form a tiny indentation below the nose on the upper lip—this makes the "bow" shape of the mouth. Let the completed face dry 2 to 3 days.

To Paint the Doll's Face

1 Paint the face with flesh-tone acrylic paint; let dry. Wash the face with a light coat of green antiquing glaze; let dry.

2 Paint the eye area with off-white acrylic paint; let dry. Paint the corneas olive green and the pupils black; let dry. Add a dot of off-white acrylic paint to the eyes to make them more life-like. Outline the eyes with a very fine line using black acrylic paint and a size 5/0 paintbrush.

3 Paint the cheeks and lips with a light wash of red acrylic paint. Let the face dry completely.

4 After the face has dried, add a final wash of brown antiquing glaze; let dry.

Attaching the Head to the Body

1 Attach the head to the body with a ⅛ x 4-inch (0.3 x 10.2 cm) long dowel.

2 Push the dowel 1 inch (2.5 cm) into the base of the head and pull out the dowel. Squirt hot glue into the hole, and then reinsert the dowel. Push the dowel down into the stuffed body about 2½ inches (6.4 cm), leaving ½ inch (1.3 cm) of the dowel exposed at her neck, again securing the dowel with hot glue.

3 Tuck the open edge of the black cotton body/neck inside and hot glue in place. *Note:* Don't worry if things don't quite line up, a crepe paper collar will cover any errors in this attachment process.

4 Hot glue the wool hair starting at the bottom portion of the head, attaching the hair in layers. Let her hair be slightly wild. Continue moving up her head, layering and attaching the hair with hot glue until you fill in the top.

To Make the Doll's Hands

1 Form the palm of the hand, the wrist, and forearm using a 2 x 1-inch (5.1 x 2.5 cm) coil of paper clay. Make the forearm at least 3 inches (7.6 cm) long so you will have plenty of area to attach it to the doll. Attach small coils of clay to the hand to make the thumb and four fingers. Smooth the clay very carefully when attaching the fingers to the hand. *Note:* I pull on the fingers and gently shape them to their exaggerated form. A witch's hands can be odd-shaped and whimsical. I purposely omitted forming a wire armature inside the hands, which is the usual method used. On this witch, the hands are small so they will be strong enough without using wire inserts, which can be tricky to do.

2 Let the paper clay pieces cure for 2 days or until completely dry.

3 Paint the hands with flesh-tone acrylic paint; let dry. Brush the hands with a light coat of green antiquing glaze; let dry.

4 Hot glue the forearm inside the black arm casing. *Note:* The blouse sleeve and the ruffled crepe cuff will cover this juncture.

To Make the Hat

1 Copy the Witch Hat and Hat Brim templates (page 123) onto cardstock and cut out shapes. Fold where marked and hot glue to secure.

2 Paint the hat with black acrylic paint; let dry. Paint the hat with a thin coat of craft glue and then sprinkle with glitter; let dry.

3 Cut a length of silver tinsel to fit around the base of the hat and hot glue to secure.

4 Cut a 2-inch (5.1 cm) circle from orange crepe paper, and a 1-inch (2.5 cm) circle from white crepe paper. Hot glue the crepe paper circles to the front of the hat then hot glue the glass bead in the center of the top circle.

To Make the Crepe Paper Collar and Wrist Embellishments

1 For the collar: Cut one 2 x 35-inch (5.1 x 88.9 cm) piece of black crepe paper. Sew a gathering stitch lengthwise down the center of the crepe paper, and pull on the thread ends to gather. Fold along the stitching line. Tie the collar around the neck using the thread ends.

2 For the wrist embellishments: Cut two 1 x 25-inch (2.5 x 63.5 cm) pieces of black crepe paper. Sew a gathering stitch lengthwise down the center of the crepe paper, and pull on the thread ends to gather. Fold the crepe paper along the stitching line. Tie one embellishment to each wrist using the thread ends.

To Make the Shawl

Cut one 10 x 10 x 18-inch (25.4 x 25.4 x 45.7 cm) triangle from an old blanket. (You also can use wool fabric.) To create the fringe, cut strips 1½ inches (3.8 cm) in from the edge of the fabric all along the perimeter. Wrap the shawl around the doll and secure in place with a vintage brooch.

To Embellish the Book

1 Paint the book with black acrylic paint; let dry. Sand the edges of the book to give it an aged appearance.

2 Copy the Book image (page 121) onto white cardstock; cut out. Using a small paintbrush, adhere the image to the front of the book with decoupage medium; let dry. Spray the book with spray sealer; let dry.

To Embellish the Doll

After completing the doll, I felt she could use a little personality. So I added vintage mismatched vegetable dye buttons I found at a flea market to Gypsy's shoes. Black buttons or different brightly colored buttons would also look good. I like them to be different sizes and styles for a folk art look.

Gypsy is sitting in a twig chair with a spider attached, but you could use a stool, wooden chair, or even a pumpkin as her prop. As a finishing touch, I hung a vintage coin purse around her neck.

Cones and Ornament images

Cones and Ornament
images *continued*

Haunted Table Scarf images
Enlarge 300%

Cone template

Enlarge 200%

Vintage Party image

Enlarge 125%

Party
Popper
images

Cat and Pumpkin Mask and Nose

Enlarge 200%

Checkerboard Paper

Pillow Pumpkin
Pillow Pumpkin Eyes
Pillow Pumpkin Nose
Pillow Pumpkin Teeth
Pillow Pumpkin Stem
Pillow Pumpkin Leaf

Enlarge 125%

Gray lines denote stitching pattern.

Pillow Spider Body

Pillow Spider Web

Enlarge 200%

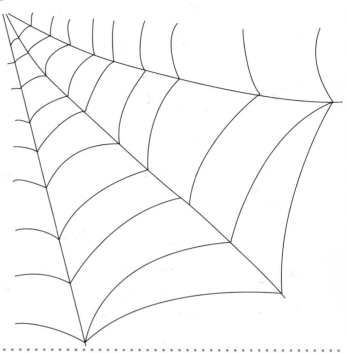

Cat Background
Cat Face
Cat Eyes
Cat Nose
Cat Mouth

Enlarge 175%

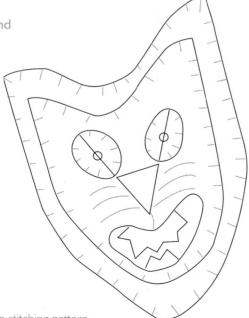

Pumpkin, Pumpkin Eyes,
Pumpkin Nose
Pumpkin Mouth
Pumpkin Stem
Pumpkin Leaf

Enlarge 175%

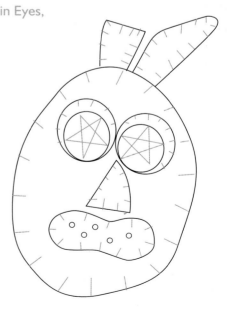

Gray lines denote stitching pattern.

Bat Background
Bat Body
Enlarge 125%

Large and Small Square
Enlarge 125%

Candy Corn Base
Candy Corn Tip
Enlarge 125%

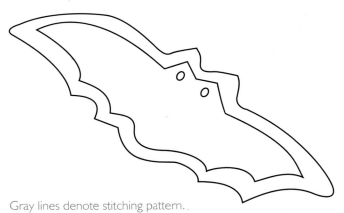

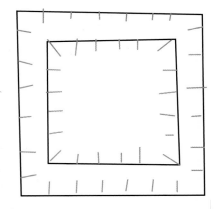

Gray lines denote stitching pattern.

Pumpkin Patch Bat

Enlarge 150%

Gray lines denote stitching pattern.

Spider Web Bat and Web

Enlarge 150%

Gray lines denote stitching pattern.

Pumpkin Vines Bat

Enlarge 150%

BOO!

Gray lines denote stitching pattern.

Bat Eyes

Bat Nose and Bat Teeth

Small Pumpkin

Large Pumpkin

Large and Small Leaves

Moon, Cat, and Fence

Enlarge 125%

Window and Ghost

Enlarge 125%

Let's Party images

Child's Vintage image

Cat, Pumpkin, and Skeleton Crepe Paper Hat images

Enlarge 125%

Party Boy Pumpkin images

Silhouette Luminary images

Enlarge 300%

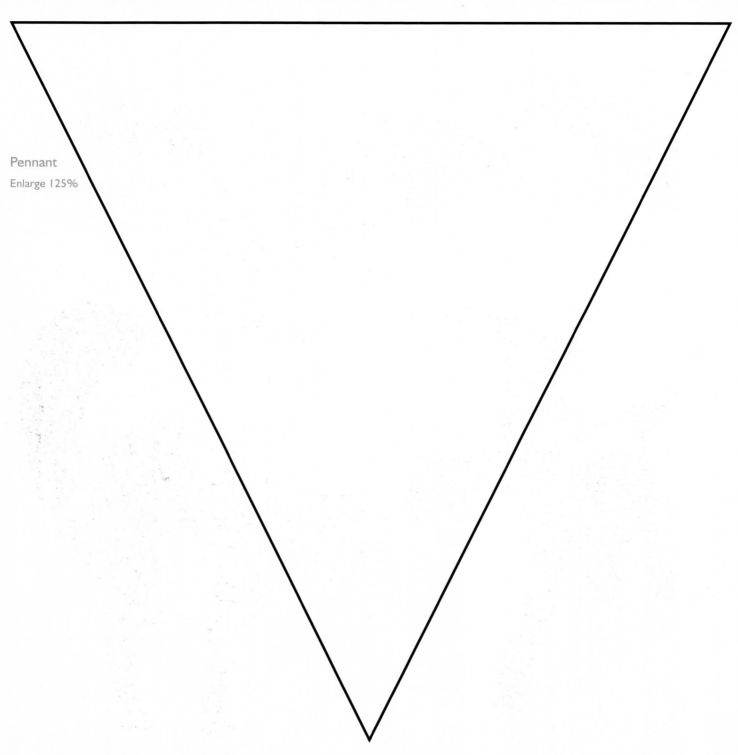

Pennant

Enlarge 125%

117

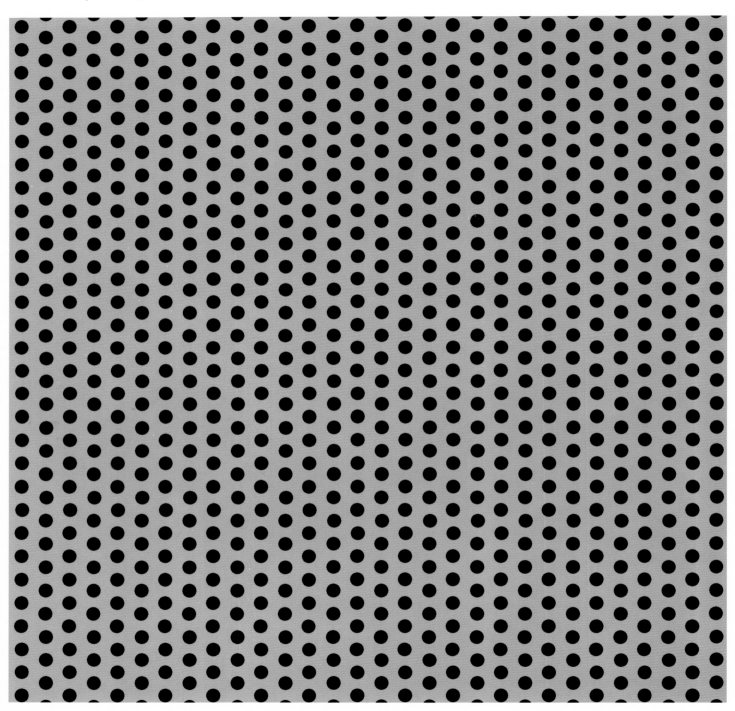

Queen images

Enlarge 200%

Postcard Luminary images

Enlarge 300%

Vintage Luminary images

Enlarge 300%

Happy Jack-O-Lantern and Scary Cat images

Enlarge 125%

Candlestick bat template

Enlarge 125%

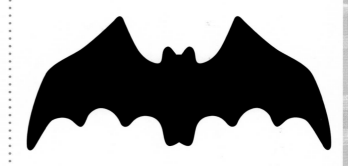

Book image

Witch Arm

Witch Leg

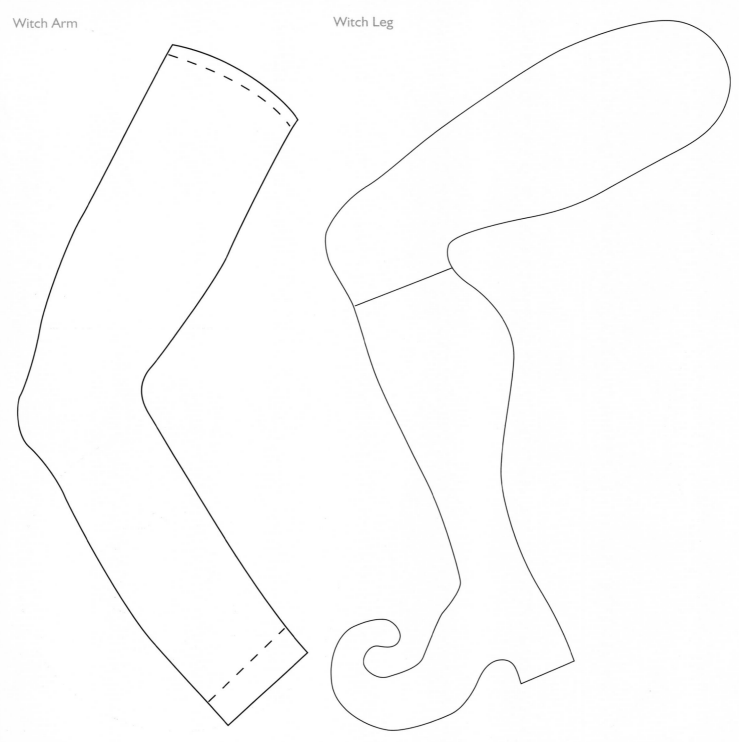

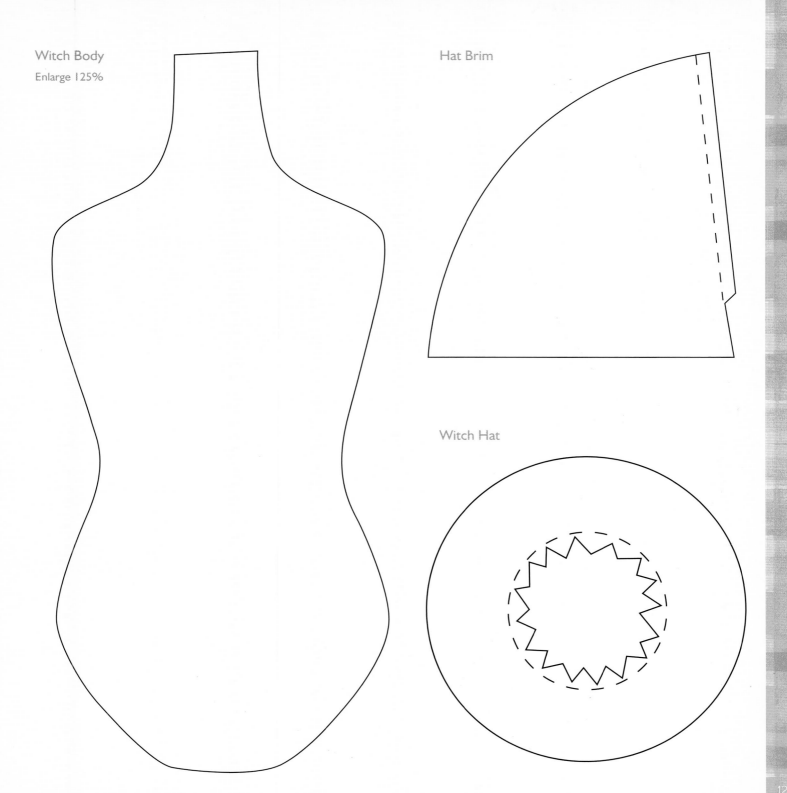

Witch Body

Enlarge 125%

Hat Brim

Witch Hat

Witch Blouse

Enlarge 125%

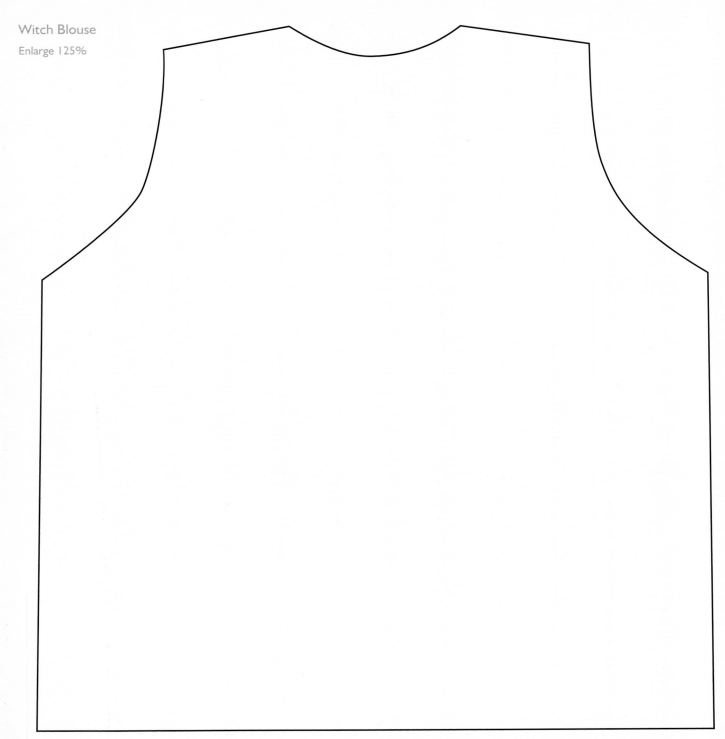

Witch Blouse Sleeve

Enlarge 125%

About the Author

Bethany Lowe is a self-taught artist whose love of antiques and holiday traditions led her into the world of design. Twenty years ago, Bethany began her career as an artist when she created her first one-of-a-kind Santa Claus figure as part of her "Nostalgia for Nicholas Collection." These designs were, and still are, based on folk art legend characters from around the world, with her most popular designs inspired by her own imagination and life experiences. Vintage robes and fabrics, antique toys, and hand-sculpted faces set her work apart. Serious collectors became enthralled with her attention to detail and supreme craftsmanship.

These early days of delivering unique designs that resonated with folk art enthusiasts quickly earned Bethany a reputation as a visionary who would take the time and effort to make things the old-fashioned way.

In 1997 Bethany decided to expand her work into other major holidays. With an artist's vision of creating unique, original, vintage-style folk art designs that are meant to enrich the holiday experience for generations, the company, Bethany Lowe Designs, was born. BLD's logo and mission statement became an invitation for the customer to "build a tradition" within their family and home.

Bethany works out of her studio on the family farm in Osco, Illinois.

Acknowledgments

Along with my husband, Curt, this book is also dedicated to my four children, Heath, Chad, Nathan, and Erin, who believed in me. They were willing to put up with a mom who baked Sculpy hands instead of cookies.

To Erin and Bonnie, two of the three stooges who helped create this book.

Thank you Bonnie B. (Brotman) for the creativity and enthusiasm you brought to the table each time we brainstormed the projects for this book. Sorry about the manicure gone black and the jack-o-lantern gone wrong by a sprinkler in the night.

Thank you Erin Glennon Lowe for encouraging me to take on this project, for organizing me along the way, and for sharing in the late-night agony of finding the perfect phrase.

Thank you Wendy Ahmad for your amazing graphic and design abilities that you are so willing to share. You are my voice to the rest of the world.

Thank you Kathy Wiegel for your technical genius in graphic design and your willingness to understand when I need an image just "one click" smaller.

Thank you Carmen Marino, another technical and graphic genius, whose cartoons on the studio dry erase board never cease to crack me up.

Thank you Sara Wheeler for your incredible talent as a seamstress. Your attention to detail always makes me look good.

Thank you Ruth Ann Newman for turning the wool projects in my head into beautiful works of art. Your love of hand embroidery shows in every stitch you take.

Thank you Connie Gallens for your incredible craftsmanship. Your talented hands create many of the accessories for my one-of-a-kind and limited-edition projects. Are you tired of making crepe paper ruffles yet?

Thank you Alexa Maciolek for quietly accepting every project task that no one else wanted to do. Sometimes the smallest tasks resonate the most.

Thank you Eli and Norah Brotman, Granny B's little grand ghouls, who provided me with the charming artwork for our little goblin's bags.

Thank you Chet Taylor, my jack-of-all-trades, who does everything with a joke and a smile.

Thank you to the rest of the BLD staff. We appreciate all of your hard work and dedication.

Special thanks to the staff at Lark and Sterling for all of their help and guidance in this endeavor, especially Rebecca Ittner and Eileen Paulin at Red Lips 4 Courage, for giving me the opportunity and for making this such an enjoyable project.

And finally, thank you Bonnie Sepaniak. No office has ever run more efficiently. You know more about my business than I do. When you retire, the doors to BLD will close forever.

Index